THE YOUNG READER

A Game Plan for Parents to Teach
Their Little Ones How to Read
and Problem Solve

Margaret Craig

PUBLISHING

missmargie519@gmail.com

ISBN: 978-0-578-77977-5 (print)
ISBN: 978-0-578-77978-2 (ebook)

Ordering Information:
Special discounts are available on quantity purchases
by corporations, associations, and others.
For details, contact missmargie519@gmail.com

Table of Contents

CHAPTER A

The Young Reader

"Trust is when your mother says to eat your salad
and you don't give it to the dog."
— *Child, age six*

So you want to help your child learn to read. Let's give it a go! While you focus on preparing your child for reading, I'll provide tips and activities to guide you on your journey together. In fact, kick-starting your child's reading can be fun when you focus on the joy of the process and use the problem-solving techniques you'll find in this book. Best of all, in learning to read, children also discover techniques that will help them solve problems throughout life—the ultimate reward for reading success.

In her book *Reading Recovery: A Guidebook for Teachers in Training*, author Marie M. Clay writes, "Reading instruction often focuses on items of knowledge—words, letters, sounds. Most children respond to this teaching in active ways. They search for links between the items and they relate new discoveries to old knowledge. They operate on print as Piaget's children operate on problems, searching for relationships which order the complexity of print and therefore simplify it."

You can make things a lot easier and simplify the process of learning to read if you help your child find those relationships—making it fun and fulfilling for both of you.

ςↄ

The cab driver asked us why we were in town. Three coworkers and I were attending a literacy conference on the East Coast, and our chatty cab driver was taking us to a local restaurant. He told us that he can't read very well: He's an actor and he memorizes his lines by using a recording. [*What?*] He said he'd repeated third grade three times because of his reading. [*What!*]

I was hoping this cab driver's story was very rare; if even only a small percentage of society has difficulty reading, it's too much. However, according to a 2019 article in the *New York Times*, two out of three children did not meet the standards for reading proficiency set by the National Assessment of Educational Progress, a test administered by the National Center for Education Statistics, the research arm of the US Department of Education.[1]

Since every learner is unique, I can't pretend to know why the cab driver couldn't read. But I can tell you what I know about teaching reading and can guide you and your child down a path with opportunities for early learning and for understanding the printed word. I have been teaching children to read for more than 25 years. I worked one-on-one with first-grade children in the Reading Recovery Council program for nine years; I guided a literacy program for grades K-5 while studying under professionals from the Teachers College Reading and Writing Project, Columbia University for five years; and I was a classroom teacher for 12 years, including four years as a middle-school teacher.

In writing this book, I began with the end in mind, writing with an understanding of how early-learning reading strategies are helpful in getting children ready for their futures as readers and students. I will provide some of the nuts and bolts behind learning to give you and your child the most benefit from your reading time together: I'll keep it simple so you won't be bogged down by all the theory about learning to read that's been developed over the years. Instead, I'll show you my 10- to 15-minute strategies that help children learn how to think about reading and how to help themselves when they're stuck.

It's fun when you spend more time in solution mode and less time in problem mode, and the main thing I want you to know is that teaching can be fun for both of you: your child wants to learn, and you want to help your child do just that. "The Young Reader," is something both of you can believe in, trust, and enjoy. *Your child can become a problem-solving thinker as you travel together down this path*. I am excited to share what I've learned from years of study and, most of all, what I've learned from children.

Are You Ready for Hands On?

Modern technology provides problem-solving opportunities for children, and I see that as a good thing. I love technology. I'm at the computer right now. But, that said, there's no technology in the chapters ahead. Instead, you'll find hands-on opportunities for learning how to read and strategies that allow you to see and understand how your child thinks.

Using these strategies, you will be an integral part of your child's development. You want your young reader to become an independent learner who processes information in creative ways that problem solve. We all experience a sense of exhilaration when we solve a problem. I've seen children grin from ear to ear when they process from left to right and figure out a new word all by themselves.

I recently witnessed an interesting adult problem-solving situation. We had a big storm that knocked out the electricity in our garage. I called the electrician who eventually solved the problem. It took many attempts, but he did not give up; he kept at it until he discovered the solution. As it turned out, the replacement ground fault circuit interrupter (GFCI) was bad, and a problem within the problem was that the outlet in the ceiling had to be checked. But how to reach it? Our garage can fit an RV, and the electrician could not reach the ceiling outlet with the ladder. So what did he do? He drove his pickup truck into the garage, set up the ladder in the bed of the truck and—voilà!—he reached the outlet. *That's problem solving. That's how you want your child to think even if it's just to figure out a word.*

Whether you are teaching a three-year-old or a 53-year-old, the process is basically the same:

- Think about what you already know and use it to help yourself.

- Spend less time on the problem and more time on the solution.

- Remember that the more you use your problem-solving skills the better you get at it.

Early Problem-Solving Skills

Most of us feel pretty darn happy with ourselves when we find a solution to a problem. So let's provide opportunities for our children to help themselves read, find solutions, and feel that exhilaration too.

Here's one early problem-solving scenario that many children experience. They crawl to a sofa or chair to pull themselves up to a standing position before they've learned to walk. You probably clap your hands and shout out words of praise. By praising them, you are validating their problem-solving skills.

You provided the avenue, the sofa, and then you helped them feel the exhilaration of success with your praise. Soon, you create an opportunity for them to take a few steps away from the support of the furniture by offering your hand. Before long they are taking baby steps without your hand. They have the desire and they are doing the work.

I think children are natural problem solvers. Some babies manage to get out of their cribs long before we would think it possible. I might want to praise that success but that would not be the safest response. Instead, I'd go the route of adjusting the sides of the crib and I'd be sure not to reprimand a child with such skills. The problem becomes mine to make things safe.

Co-Problem Solving

When children cannot yet problem-solve for themselves in a situation, you can model problem-solving for them. What does this mean? Well, when you think out loud, you are modeling. Let's say you throw a ball and they miss catching it. Most likely you talk about it, then you show them a possible solution like moving closer to the toss or using a bigger ball or a better way to hold their hands. In these early years you are co-problem-solving with your children; eventually they will take off and problem-solve on their own. Problem-solving in reading is just as exciting. *If children learn to problem-solve as they learn to read, they won't have a problem reading.*

Getting Ready to Be Ready to Read

Readiness is a developmental state of mind and body that applies to many areas of life. You'll see it repeatedly throughout children's physical development. They can't chew until they have teeth. They can't run before they can walk. They can't drink from a cup on their own before their hands can hold onto the cup. And they don't say "dada" or "mama" before they're ready.

Brain development and stages of readiness are not as easy to discern as signs of physical development and readiness. We have to look carefully for signs of mental and emotional readiness. Tears and negative behavior are signs that often mean, "I'm not ready!" (Unless they mean, "I need a nap!") Smiles, willingness, eagerness, and listening are signs that most often say, "I'm ready!"

The website *healthychildren.org*, has this to say about reading readiness. "Is your child interested in learning the names of letters? Does he look through books and magazines on his own? Does he like to "write" with a pencil or pen? Does he listen attentively during story time? If the answer is "yes," he may be ready to learn some of the basics of reading. If not, he's like most preschoolers, and will take another year or two to develop the language skills, visual perception, and memory he needs to begin formal reading."

You can read more at: www.healthychildren.org/English/ages-stages/preschool/Pages/Is-Your-Child-Ready-to-Read.aspx

A Readiness Challenge

Yesterday was a beautiful sunny day and I thought it would be healthy for my six-month-old dog, Gus, and me to go for a nice long walk. So off we went.

Well, either my 61-pound puppy wasn't ready, or I wasn't ready. We plodded on for a good mile, stopping occasionally. He pulled and darted, pulled and darted, sniffed and pulled, and sniffed and darted. My hands and arms are still recovering from their exercise in maximum strength resistance.

When we finally arrived home I was frustrated and grumpy. I was just trying to be a good dog mom and do the all-American dog-owner thing on a beautiful day. I did everything right, right? Wrong! Gus wasn't ready for such a l-o-o-o-n-g walk.

Of course, a puppy is very different from a child, but you get the idea. Struggle, struggle, struggle is a sign of taking on a task too soon.

Readiness Elements

Potty training and learning to ride a bicycle and coloring inside the lines all have a readiness element. *Not only do children need to be physically and intellectually ready for the challenge, they have to have some interest in it.*

If we suspect our children are ready to learn something new, we can make or break the success of the experience with our attitude and words. That's where our readiness as parents plays an important role in our children's successful learning experiences. I try to be in the best mood possible when I'm teaching, especially if I'm teaching something new.

Mood Matters

Children are very sensitive to our feelings and moods. Try to find the zone where you and your child are excited and eager to interact as teacher and student. Yes, I'm calling you a teacher because that's what you are, a teacher of many, many, things.

If any of the activities I suggest cause frustration or tension between you and your child, stop and try again another time. Find a way to end the activity on a happy note so that both you and your child will look forward to trying it again later on. *Children learn faster and have more fun if we teach what they are ready to learn when they are ready to learn it.*

Follow the Learner's Readiness

When we pay attention to and follow the learner's readiness, the process is fun and children learn. If we try to teach our children something they're not yet ready to learn, we set ourselves up for frustration and maybe even disappointment. Certainly we don't want our children to feel we are disappointed in them, especially if we've been plodding on, trying to teach something that they weren't ready for at the time.

Select the Right Activity

Knowing how to select the right activity for the right time is a bit of a guessing game at first, but you know your child best. You will be able to tell if they are happy and enjoying whatever activity you are engaging in with them.

Make a Lesson Easy and Fun

It's always fun when an activity or lesson is easy for us to teach and for children to learn. I have found, in teaching many children to read, that it's better that an activity be a little too easy than a little too hard. So, whether you are sitting down to read a story, sing the "ABC song," play with letter blocks, or sort squares, circles, rectangles, and ovals, have fun!

Telling and Asking

Let me share a useful tip for teaching your little students: There's a "telling" part of teaching where we give information to a child, and there's an "asking" part of teaching where we ask for information from a child. The reason we ask is not to trick them, but to help engage them beyond just listening.

Here's the tricky part for you: Try your best to ask children questions that you are sure they can answer. Being able to answer the questions will help to keep them excited about learning to read.

For instance, you might ask your child, "What's this word?" making sure it's a word they know. Children love to make you happy by coming up with the right answer. It will build their confidence and they will be excited about learning.

Ready to Engage

The information and the activities I share in this book are useful for children at every age, from birth on up. It's not possible to specify at what age a child will be ready to engage in the different strategies and activities that are involved in learning to read. Every child is different and will be ready for different things at different age levels. Moms and dads generally know best.

Teaching Tools

Here are the basic things you'll need to teach enjoyably.

- A place where you can work together for 10 or 15 minutes: the kitchen table, a sofa, a desk, or a place to sit on the floor will do just fine

- A quiet uninterrupted time, if possible

- A good attitude and happy mood are a must

- Post-it Notes and index cards

- A basket of books

- A whiteboard and a dry-erase marker and eraser

- Magnetic letters: my favorites are Quercetti magnetic letters. (Note: upper- and lower-case letters are available on Amazon.)

Now, get ready to do what your child is already thinking— The Young Reader!

CHAPTER B

Sorting Socks

"How do you spell H?"
—Child, age six

"How do you spell H?" Now what kind of a question is that? It makes me chuckle inside. The question suggests to me that the child doesn't yet know the difference between a word and a letter. Just a simple confusion. Or perhaps she knew the difference but didn't know that the word "letter" refers to one of the ABCs. Maybe she thought all letters and words are called "words."

Imagine sitting in a classroom and the teacher is talking about letters and you think she is talking about words. Or imagine the teacher talking about words and you think she is talking about letters. Oh my! You might raise your hand and say that you don't understand unless you are only five- or six-years old, in which case you might just start daydreaming about something else altogether.

How Can We Help?
You can help your child recognize the differences between things by having short conversations. Simply talking about

similarities and differences between things as you come across them in daily life is helpful.

In this situation, there's no need to discuss what's wrong about confusing a letter and a word, simply talk about the difference between a letter and a word. And it's not necessary to discuss and teach immediately after noticing that your child is confused. Take some think time and then discuss.

Hands-On Solutions

To help the child who asked me how to spell H, we talked about the difference between a letter and a word. Then I prepared a dozen index cards with words and letters on them. I made six cards with one letter on each: **P, G, A, B, S,** and **T.** I knew she knew those letters. Then I made six cards with one word on each: **cat, mom, am, me, go,** and **stop.** I shuffled the cards and asked her to put the cards with a letter in one pile and the cards with a word in another. Success. It was easy and it was hands-on. *Easy, hands-on activities make learning fun and kick things up a notch from just talking about a subject.*

Sorting Is Key

When we sort things, whether it's words or silverware, we separate according to type and put similar items into groups. Noticing differences and sameness is what we do as we sort.

You and I sort without much thought. It comes naturally to us now. We've learned it over time from our parents, teachers, and by observing others. We put the forks in one slot, the knives in another, and the spoons in a third slot. We sort summer clothes from winter clothes. We put bath towels in one pile and washcloths in another. My husband sorts nails and various tools in the garage. The list of things we sort is endless.

We also sort as we read. Noticing and understanding differences is an important part of becoming a reader. If we teach our children to sort at an early age, we are actually teaching them a strategy that is important in teaching them to read.

Sorting is an excellent way to spend enjoyable time together while, at the same time, preparing your child to learn to read. The ability to notice the differences between letters and words can help avoid confusions as they learn

Good readers sort automatically with ease. For example, the words **not** and **hot, take** and **bake**, are different at the beginning but the same after that. The words **ship** and **shop**, are the same at the beginning and at the end, but different in the middle.

There are subtle differences in letters and words, but you can get your child ready to notice those subtle differences by beginning with sorting large objects that have obvious differences, like different pairs of shoes, or pennies and nickels, or big toys and little toys. It's a bit like the concept that large motor skills—like walking and running—develop before small motor skills—like using a fork and coloring inside the lines. *Developing sorting skills by using objects around the house is meaningful, useful, and surprisingly easy.*

Use What You Already Have on Hand

Maybe your child is already sorting. Some toys have easy-to-recognize sorting characteristics like shapes or colors. You can sort toy cars by size or by color or by style—sedan, truck, and recreational vehicle. You can sort barrettes by color. You can sort socks by size or by color. Sort into piles or baskets or drawers. Sort on the floor, on the table, in the yard, whatever works in your home.

Show Your Child How to Sort While They Watch

- Start by sorting something yourself.

- Model the activity for children by talking about what you are doing as you sort.

- Do the activity together. You might need to do this several times.

- When ready, children can do the sorting activity themselves. Cheer them on with praise and high-fives!

Mini List of Things to Sort		
Socks	Toy Cars	Playing Cards
Barrettes	Legos	Washed Laundry
Letters	Buttons	Sea Shells
Words	Coins	Rocks

Sorting with Specific Reading Skills in Mind

Many of the things that might be confusing in learning to read can be avoided by noticing difference and similarities, especially when noticing them becomes automatic. Noticing more subtle differences and similarities comes into play with letters. The differences are just smaller in size and detail.

For example, look at the letters **h, n,** and **r**. They all are made with a stick and a curve. The parts of **h, n,** and **r** that are different are a short stick versus a long stick, and a partial curve versus a curve that goes all the way down. They can be easy to confuse for a new reader. *Time for a strategy activity.* A strategy activity is a plan of action to help young children process information and learn skills on their path to becoming readers.

Strategy Activity

- Gather Post-it Notes, index cards, or cut up pieces of paper.

- Write an **n** on five sheets, an **r** on five sheets, and an **h** on five sheets. Be sure to write neatly and both dark and large enough that the letters are easy to read.

- Shuffle the sheets of paper and ask your child to make three piles, one pile for each of the letters. If you use Post-it notes, it's fun to stick them, scrambled, on a wall, and ask your child to find all the letter **n** notes, then the **h** notes etc.

Sorting Activities

All children have things that confuse them as they learn to read, and those things differ from child to child. Sorting is one way to de-confuse, encouraging recognition by putting like things together. So many everyday things can be sorted. With a little creativity, I know you'll have success with it, it's a simple and enjoyable process.

Pick One Letter

Here's an example of what I would do to help if a child is confusing **b** and **d**. Start by picking one, the **b** or the **d**. If you focus on both letters at the same time, it's like having two connected train engines going in opposite directions: trying hard but stuck in one place. Help your child to master the look and sound of each of the letters, one at a time. When they've mastered one, they'll know the other isn't it.

If your child has a **b** or **d** in his name, I would choose that letter. If his name is Ted or Aiden or Donald or Jared, for instance, work on mastering the d. If there is no d in the name, teach and talk about words that have a d in different positions—beginning, middle, and end. Words like **and, do,** and **ride**.

Get out your magnetic letters. Put the letter **d** on the refrigerator by itself, then write out your chosen words using the **d**.

If the child's name is Debra, there's a **b** in the middle. If you call her Deb, the **b** is at the end. If there is no **b** in your child's name, teach and talk about words that have a **b** in different positions within the word, words like **big, baby,** and **tub**. Put the magnetic letter b on the refrigerator by itself and then spell out the chosen words, using the **b**.

This is a different kind of sorting, one that asks children to focus on one thing at a time. By mastering each letter, children will have a specific point of reference when they need to help themselves in reading or writing.

Keep It Easy, Brief, and Fun—and Don't Forget to Talk

Remember to keep activities easy and fun. The activities I've detailed here take only five or ten minutes and, hopefully, they will be enjoyable. Having a conversation with your child about what you are doing as you practice the activity will also be helpful.

Don't forget, these activities are not tests. They are all fun and beneficial for learning to read and for getting to know a little more about your child. Whether sorting socks or sorting letters, the goal is to have fun while teaching a key skill on the journey to raising a reader.

CHAPTER C

Over, Under, Beginning, End

"Don't say "ain't" or you'll get called Billy Joe Bob."
—Child, age six

This question appeared on a third-grade test: Which word has the same beginning sound as **fast**?

a. book   c. farmer

b. stop   d. table

Marissa chose **table** as her answer. I knew she was a good student and I thought it was odd that she would get that wrong. The answer, of course, is **farmer**. After talking with her about this, I realized she didn't understand the meaning of the word "beginning."

This was a real wake-up call for me. How often does something like this happen in a child's early learning years? Who would have thought that a third-grade student might not understand the meaning of the word "beginning?"

Learning from Marissa, I realized the importance of understanding directional words. Shortly afterward, I met with a small group of kindergarten boys for a reading lesson. I asked them to turn to the first page of a book I'd given each of them. The unsure look on their faces was more evidence of the importance of teaching the meaning of these words early in a child's life. The boys were not sure exactly what I meant by the *first* page. Perhaps the problem was more common than I had thought.

During those years, most of my work day was spent with first-grade children, teaching them specifically to read and write. I began paying more attention to my conversations with them, and I carefully—and frequently—used the words and phrasing listed here to model and teach words used in giving directions.

Common Words and Phrases for Understanding Directions		
in front of	at the beginning	beside
next to	at the end	under
on top of	next	bottom
before	after	
beneath	first	
last	middle	

Directional Activity

Spell out your child's name with magnetic letters or write it on a piece of paper. You'll use the name as a starting point to find out what your child knows and teach what they don't know about directions. You'll do this by asking a few simple questions that include directional words that you think your child will know how to answer.

For example:

Can you count the letters **in** your name?

Can you slide your finger **under** your name?

Can you put your finger **under** the **first** letter of your name?

Can you put your finger **under** the **second** letter of your **first** name?

Can you put your finger **under** the **last** letter of your **first** name?

Can you tell me what letter is at the **beginning** of your **first** name?

The best policy is to ask only questions that your child knows the answer to, or ones you think they know. *Remember that asking questions they can answer boosts their confidence and makes them hungry for more.*

Children tend to want to quit things rather quickly if they don't feel successful. Watch for disappointed looks—these will tell you when children feel badly about not doing something right or disappointing you when they get something wrong. If that happens, jump in with a quick reinforcement of praise, "It's great how you're taking some time to think before giving me the answer." Then provide the answer or a helpful clue to the answer, to help keep them engaged and ready to try again.

Words and Phrases Specific to a Book

the page

the cover

the front of the book

the back of the book

top of the page

middle of the page

bottom of the page

under the picture

A good time to teach a few book concepts is when you sit down with your child to read a book that you've read before and that you both know and love. Talking about words and phrases specific to the layout of a book won't detract from following the storyline if you choose a book that is already familiar.

Be aware that confusions can occur and keep an eye out for your child's clear understanding of the words and phrases I've listed above. This will help you guide your child's grasp of these early learning-to-read concepts.

Try to discuss directional words in different situations. For example, children are apt to know what it means to be **first in line** to go to lunch, but they might need a little instruction in the use of **first** in other situations, like the **first letter in a word** or the **first page of a book**.

It's a good idea to show, model, or demonstrate these concepts in different situations as they come up throughout the day until we're sure our children understand. *We don't want to assume they understand, we want to know they understand.*

Baby Talk and Clear Speech

"I'm trying to **contrate***."* *"Football is cool. I never go out of* ***bounce***.*"

I agree that toddlers and preschool children sound so cute with their babyish speech. It just happens naturally as they learn to use new words. However, sometimes their mispronunciation of words can be due, in part, to our own speech or diction. It's best if we speak clearly and distinctly to our children.

We try to set a good example in many areas, such as manners, healthy eating, and what we watch on television. How we speak to our children and to others is another area for setting a good example. *Incorrect or muffled speech can cause challenges in learning to read.*

Just to be clear, I am not talking about speech impediments here. I am referring to mispronunciations: words that children say incorrectly because they don't know the correct pronunciation.

Think about **wif** instead of **with** for a child learning to read. The word **with** is a good example that makes my point because the **th** sound appears in so many words! Understanding that the two letters make one sound is very important and not always easy to grasp: it's particularly confusing for a child trying to learn to read the word **with** if he pronounces it as **wif**.

Another word that is easily mispronounced is **for**, which is often pronounced as **fer**. We speak so quickly that **fer** goes unnoticed. However, correct pronunciation will be very helpful to a beginning reader.

Children learn their words by listening to the adults around them. The communication and language process begins with listening when we are born, to be followed by speech, then reading and writing. In the end, it all depends on communicating and learning from each other.

The bottom line for us as teachers:

- Speak clearly.

- Send children to school with an understanding of directional words.

I know this sounds so basic and easy, but my experience tells me *we sometimes assume children know basic things when, in fact, they don't know them—yet.*

CHAPTER D

Bridge the Letter to Word Gap

"I had to wash my apple. A girl touched it."
—Child, age six

My jaw dropped the day I walked by a bulletin board in a school hall that displayed pictures of famous people with dyslexia:

Albert Einstein: theoretical physicist

Keira Knightley: English actress

Steve Jobs: founder of Apple

Muhammad Ali: legendary heavyweight boxing champ

Henry Winkler: actor/author

Jewel: American singer-songwriter

The Mayo Clinic defines dyslexia as, "A learning disorder that involves difficulty reading due to problems identifying speech sounds and learning how they relate to letters and words (decoding). Also called reading disability, dyslexia affects areas of the brain that process language."

After the shock of seeing those names wore off, my thoughts jumped to this: "A Reading Recovery teacher could have helped all of those people. It's too bad that every school can't have a fully implemented Reading Recovery program. Why do kids who struggle with reading get pulled out of the classroom to be given remedial help from paraprofessionals who are not trained teachers?"

"What the child needs to know is a few items and some strategies for picking up new ones later, as he reads."— Marie M. Clay, 1926–2007, distinguished researcher known for her work in educational literacy and founder of the Reading Recovery Program.[2]

Okay, so let's do our best to be the parents who know how to help our children learn to read.

Let's start with teaching a few letters

Teach the Letter M
- Talk about the letter.

- Show the letter by writing it on a piece of paper, on a whiteboard, or by pointing it out in a book, such as an ABC book.

- If you have a magnetic letter **m**, have your child hold it, look at it, and say its name. Make it feel like this is something cool to know about.

Have fun and play games with the letter, maybe putting it in your child's shoe, so when they go to put on the shoe you can act surprised and say, "Oh look! There's an **m**!" Or, "Oh look! It's a letter. Do you know what letter this is? This is the one that sounds like "mmmmmm."

Use Post-its

I love using Post-its for early learning activities. Write a single letter on each of a dozen or so Post-its, making five of them the letter **m**. Write the letters large enough for emphasis. Stick the Post-its on the wall and ask your child to find the ones that have a letter **m**.

Children seem to love doing this. It's especially good for children who don't want to sit still for very long. Another way to pose the question is to ask your child to find the letters that make the sound "mmmmm."

Because you know your child well, you can adjust the activity to suit their understanding of letters. Make a game of it, using words instead of letters. Ask your child to find a certain word and then another and then another. I know you can be creative with this activity.

Play "I See Something" with Letters and Sounds

You have probably heard of the game "I See Something," also known as "I Spy." One person says, "I see something blue," and the others playing the game try to guess which object in the room that might be.

You can kick it up a notch and say, "I see something that starts with a **p**," or "I see something that starts with an **m**." Choose the letter based on which letters and sounds your child knows. As they try to guess the object, you'll get information on whether or not they know a particular sound. This is a fun way to start a conversation about letters and sounds.

Write Words and Letters on a Whiteboard

Another tool for teaching and talking about letters and words is the whiteboard. Be sure to use dry-erase markers on your whiteboard because permanent markers will ruin it. Write a letter or word on the board and talk about it. Or, write a letter and have your child trace over it with the dry-erase marker after you talk about it.

I like whiteboards better than chalkboards, because there's no chalk-dust mess. Some whiteboards are also magnetic and you can use them to make words with magnetic letters. It's fun to sit next to your child on the sofa and talk about words and letters, how they go together, and what they sound like.

Putting the three letters **m**, **o**, and **m** in your closed hand, say, "Let's make the word **mom**. What sound do you hear coming out of your mouth first when you say **mom**? Say it slowly." If your child says **mmm**, put down the **m**, and say, "Yes, and that sound is the sound of the letter **m**." With the **m** on the board, talk about other words that start with **m** and listen for the sound. Say the words, **me, man, mop,** and listen for the **m** sound.

Put the **om** next to the **m** and say, "That's the word mom. I like the way you helped me get it started with the **m**."

Give O a Try

Putting **o** and **n** in your closed hand say, "Let's make the word **on**. What sound do you hear coming out of your mouth first when you say **on**? Say it slowly." If your child makes the sound of **o**, say, "Yes, and that sound is the sound of **o**." With the **o** on the board, talk about other words that start with o and listen for the sound. Say the words, **octopus, owl, olive,** and listen for the sound of **o**. Then put the **n** next to the **o** and say, "That's the word **on**. I like the way you helped me get **on** started with the **o**."

Short **o** is a good sound to know because it is very often the second letter in a word. Some of those words are **mom, mop, cot, hot, sock, pop, rock,** just to give you a few.

I'm guessing your child knows other letters as well, but it is through conversation with our children that we learn what they know. Sometimes simply asking them if they know any other letters will provide a surprise answer. Children learn letters from television shows like *Sesame Street*. Sometimes they learn from other children. Maybe you have taught the "ABC song" and they know some of the letters from the song.

Moving On to A

Using the same activity, the next letter and sound I would teach is the **short a**. Start with making the word **am**. A few other words to help with this activity are **and, ask, apple.** There's a method to this! I'm setting things up so that we can show a child how words work, and also how to use something they already know to figure out something new.

So now your child knows **m, o, a**. With these three letters you can make the words **mom, mam, am**. You can write the words on the whiteboard, make them with magnets, write them on paper, or use Post-its on the wall.

Adding to the list, you can then teach the letter **h**. Put it in front of **am** and you have **ham**. Many words like these match the sound coming out of our mouths. The sounds can be easily heard and identified if we say the word slowly.

Say the first sound distinctly and then soften the rest of the sounds and say them slowly. Say, "haaammm." When you say the words slowly, you can hear what letter comes next. Continue to build, teaching new letters, what they sound like, and how they can be used to make words. Children will eventually know all the letters and sounds, and because they know how the letters and sounds go together, they will be able to figure out some new words on their own.

Easy Words to Play With and Talk About

Here are some easy words to play with as your child learns more letters and sounds. Talk about them and how the letters and sounds come together to make words: **am, man, at, cat, mat, can, will, me, my, it, I, he, did, a, not, is**.

Talking about words with your child really helps understanding. This is especially true with words that do not exactly match the sounds coming out of our mouths. Many of these are words we use all the time and are important to know. These include words in which two letters—like **th** or **sh**—make one sound, or where there are silent letters. Here are some examples: **the, look, with, this, will, she, her, love, like, come, light, could, all, they**.

When children are in kindergarten and first grade they are often required to know lists of words used with high frequency that are called **sight words**. Sight words are usually learned by memorization, which is fine; the more words they know the better, but I am shooting for something beyond memorizing here.

Get a Word Started

Something you can do that is sure to help is to show your child how to get a word started. If a child gets stuck on a word, the first thing I would say is, "Can you get the word started?" Or "Put your finger under the first letter and get it started." Once they know how to do this, all you have to say is, "What can you do to help yourself?"

One thing I hope every child can learn to do is to put their finger under the first letter of a word and get it started. There's no starting in the middle or at the end! Next, they will learn to slowly slide their finger under the word. Their finger guides their eyes in a left-to-right direction. When the eyes can move left to right without the guide of the finger it's okay to stop using the finger guide.

Kicking It Up a Notch

We are helping our children go from letters to words, from words to sentences, and from sentences to stories; it's a process. We're teaching more than item knowledge.

It can be quite a challenge to find very-early-learning reading materials, such as books, so I made my own. If you decide to make your own, be sure to use words that your child knows and include pictures as well. Here are some examples:

I once had a student come to my classroom for reading help who had a great deal of memorized information at his fingertips. He had great item knowledge. He knew every letter of the alphabet, every sound those letters made, and a nice list of sight words. But he had no idea how to put all of that together into what we call reading.

Children who move from one school to another sometimes miss important pieces of the process of learning how to read, and that was his situation. *If you show children the process, along with small amounts of item knowledge, you'll be the hero behind their success at learning to read.*

I've never met a child who didn't want to learn to read—so let's do this! With your help, your child will learn letters and words and how they come together to entertain us and inform us in books. Have fun with this. Remember to praise your child and pat yourself on the back for the great job you are doing.

CHAPTER E

The Magic of Storytime

"I have a big brother and a middle-sized sister."
— Child, age six

You already know that reading to your children is a big deal. So, let's take a look at how to enrich the experience for both of you. For example, how can the pictures enrich the experience? How do stories provide opportunities for problem-solving conversations? How can you be sure your child is comprehending what you're reading?

The Early Years

In their early years, your children will love the sound of your voice and the attention you give them when you sit down to read a story together. Some mothers even read to their baby while still in the womb. Children's books often have a nice, slow rhythm, and while babies don't understand the story, they feel the rhythm and the mood. Reading time is a happy time and perhaps a falling-asleep time.

What's Your Mood?

As the months and years roll on, establishing the right mood or setting for reading a story can be a little trickier. In your busy day, finding the time when the listener and the reader are both in the right mood can be a challenge. Just do the best you can. *You will both enjoy the experience more when you find that just-right moment in time.*

There is no formula for choosing the right time to read to your child. It's a personality thing as well as a time-management situation. For some it will be bedtime, for some it will be after breakfast, for some it will be when mommy gets home from work. We often hear the phrase "bedtime stories," but there's no need to take that to heart. *Read when it works best for both you and your child.*

Depending on your child's age and personality, I suggest reading from five to twenty minutes at a sitting. Sometimes children just want five minutes of togetherness with you and then they're ready to go back to doing their own thing. What's really cool though, is that children will begin to associate books and reading with cozy happy feelings.

Creating an Atmosphere for Reading

We talked about mood, now let's talk about atmosphere. While toys may seem to take over a child's bedroom, books are just as important and deserve a significant place where you and your young reader can put your hands on just the story you're looking for. A bookcase in the bedroom helps to create a reading atmosphere and allows your child to choose a favorite bedtime book. A book basket in the family room is as inviting as a toy basket and suggests an atmosphere where books are a pleasure to open and enjoy at playtime or any time.

The book basket in the family room would be my choice: have it sitting on the floor so your child can walk over and grab a book to look through anytime, whether just to look at the pictures or to read it aloud with you. *Children need books in their environment to learn to love to read just as they need water to learn to swim.*

Love for a Specific Book

Even as babies, our children develop preferences; they know what they like and what they don't like. Sometimes we have a heck of a time figuring out what those likes and dislikes are. Other times, such as with food choices—when they spit out the squash but gobble the custard—it's obvious. It can be almost this obvious with book choices too. You'll notice that certain books really hold their attention—other books, not so much. Brilliant little people that they are, they are developing preferences of all kinds every day.

When children are too young to communicate through conversation, they find other ways to let us know their preferences. Perhaps simply handing you a book is their request for you to read a particular story that they really like. Perhaps crying when you put the book away is a request for more. It's such a joy to be in on it, to watch them express their individuality.

You might be one of those parents who, at some point, finds it necessary to hide a particular book because it's become such a favorite that you're sure you'll have to go somewhere and scream if you read it again. A friend of mine found herself hiding the book *Goodnight Moon* from her little girl, Morgan. Morgan was 16 months old and she already chose it as her favorite. She would get the book out of the book basket and carry it to Mommy or Daddy and make her request using her best vocabulary. She knew the word, "again." It makes me chuckle.

Rather than finding a place to scream, or banishing Goodnight Moon altogether, Morgan's parents solved the problem by hiding the book and then lovingly bringing it out for reading once or twice a day. Morgan gets what she craves, and Mom and Dad's sanity is saved.

Perhaps it was the way Mom and Dad read the book that delighted Morgan. Perhaps it was the language and rhythm of the author's words that appealed to her. *Hearing language comes before speaking language, and speaking comes before reading and before writing.* This big bundle of communication is enhanced and grows as we talk and read to our children.

Choosing Books to Put in the Basket

In the beginning, book selection is a guessing game. Trial and error is unavoidable. Be sure to choose books that have illustrations to help tell the story. Great pictures help to hold children's interest and they also help give meaning to the story. Some children prefer nonfiction over fiction; give them a taste of both. Books about sharks or snakes or baseball are informative and interesting. Fictional stories give insight into relationships and life.

Visit a Bookstore or Library with Your Child

I love going to the children's section in a bookstore. The best and most beautiful books are often displayed on tables and shelves to help us in our search. The people who work there can help direct you to new titles or special subject areas. It's such a fun place.

I also love going to the children's section of the local library. It has comfy places to sit and look through books. The librarians are knowledgeable and helpful. They can give you suggestions for interesting books to check out and put in your family-room book basket.

Many libraries also have a regularly-scheduled story hour when the librarian reads aloud to children who are gathered around, sitting on their parents' laps. Some libraries offer a story hour for children as young as nine-months-old. You may need to register for these events so that the library knows how many children to expect. Story hour is awesome! And it's free!

Browse Books Online Together

It's fun to search for books online. You and your little one can browse together, searching for books on subjects you find interesting. Most online vendors offer a "look inside" feature so that you can check out the first few pages before deciding to make a purchase.

YouTube offers a huge selection of children's books that are read aloud with a full view of the pages and pictures. Enter "children's books" in the search section of YouTube and you will be pleasantly surprised by the selection offered for your viewing and entertainment.

How to Read to a Wiggle Worm

Have you ever heard anyone say that watching baseball on TV is like watching paint dry? I have. Many times. I'm thinking that's a little bit what it's like for children to sit and listen to a story if they have no idea what we're talking about: wiggle, wiggle. Wiggling begins when children are not active participants. Here are several ways to engage them:

- **Share the choice:** Grab children's interest by involving them in the book choice. Choice is empowering. Hold up two or three books and ask which one they would like you to read. Because you made the initial choice and they made the final choice, you both end up having some say in choosing the book. It only makes sense that children will want to pay attention to a book that they chose.

- **Share pictures together first:** It's a good practice for you and your child to look at the pictures in a new book together before you read the story for the first time. Sometimes children are so engrossed in the pictures that they don't listen to the words. If you go through the illustrations first, talking about what the pictures are about, children will listen more closely to the story. You will help to develop comprehension skills through the use of pictures and words.

- **Have conversations:** The pictures help to provide opportunities for little conversations. *Ask your child questions that they can easily answer.* A good question to start a conversation might be, "I like...on this page. What do you like?" Another might be, "I think...What do you think?" You can have these conversations while looking at the pictures, at some point during the reading or after you have finished reading.

- **Don't forget to respond:** It's a good practice to acknowledge children's responses. After they say what they like or think, you can respond with something positive like:

  I like that, too!

  You're such a good thinker!

  Why do you like that?

  Why do you think that?

  That's wonderful!

- **Practice listening:** Looking and talking about pictures is a big language experience for your child. It is also a window into learning how they think and what they think. Be prepared for some surprises. You will learn what your child notices, what gets their attention, what's important, and what you might need to teach or explain. Pictures bring about good conversation at an early age. Both of you will have practice at listening and talking.

- **Divide the process:** Depending on how much time you have, you can check out the pictures during one sitting and read the story at another. This gives you both something to look forward to: another time of togetherness when you read the story. If you do the reading at a second sitting, refresh everyone's memory by quickly looking at the pictures again—then let the reading begin!

- **Praise is always welcome:** Remember to praise or compliment your child during and after your time together. Here are a few ideas. I'm sure you'll find even more rewarding things to say:

> You're such a good listener!

> I love reading to you and listening to what you have to say!

> This is a really good book that you chose.

> Thank you for helping me hold the book.

Reading Stories with Problems and Solutions

Some children's books give us opportunities to point out good problem-solving ideas. For instance, after reading *The Three Little Pigs*, we could say, "It sure was a good idea to build a house of bricks so the big bad wolf couldn't blow it down." Not all stories have problem-solving scenarios, but be on the lookout for them where they do occur, and be sure to talk about them. There is a wonderful feeling of satisfaction that comes with solving a problem. Pointing out solutions in stories can help develop solution-oriented thinking in our children.

Can I Just Read the Book?

Of course you can just read a book straight through with no conversation. Sometimes that's what the mood calls for. It's a good way to develop listening skills and just following the story might be what your child prefers, especially if it's a book that you read again and again.

Sometimes you might be just too tired to do the conversation and teaching thing. Remember you have choices: You can read a book using the pictures and conversation to support comprehension; You can highlight problem solving in stories; Or you can read a book straight through, no talking, and develop good listening skills. You decide. Above all, have fun!

CHAPTER F

This Is a Shoe.
This Is an A.

"My dog sleeps in the liver room."
—*Child, age six*

What does your child already know? Is literacy a part of your child's life?

Some school districts have kindergarten testing. The administration and teaching staff want to find out what your child already knows so that they know where to start teaching. I have participated in such testing; it can be stressful for parents and children who haven't made literacy part of the beginning years in their child's life. However, the process can also be fun for children who are confident and who like demonstrating what they know. Let me show you some ways to help you and your child be in this confident group.

You might begin by calling the school district your child will be attending and asking if they do kindergarten testing (sometimes referred to as kindergarten screening). You can also ask what your child will be asked to do during the testing.

ABC Testing

The kindergarten testing that I participated in involved testing knowledge of upper-case letters separately from lower-case letters. In both sets, the letters were not in sequence. The instructions were to point your finger under each letter and say the name of the letter. Does your child know how to do this? It starts with teaching the alphabet.

B E T M C A D L Y H U

F N P O S W G I J K Q Z R V X K

a c t k g r I s x m b

p y e x v

d q f w z h j o I u

Start Teaching the Alphabet

You may be wondering when and how we begin teaching our children the alphabet. Look at it this way, when children are very young, we teach the word "shoe." We show them a shoe and say the word "shoe" and they say "shoe." Soon it becomes something they know. You are a teacher!

A shoe is something you see every day and a word you can teach every day until it's known. In the same way, creating an atmosphere that includes letters and books and shapes and colors makes it fun and easy to teach your children the ABCs. *If children see these things every day and you call them by name and talk about them, recognizing letters and shapes and colors becomes as easy as recognizing a shoe and knowing what it's called.*

We don't need to learn the theories of cognitive development to teach our children beginning literacy. It's helpful, however, to have some good learning tools to get us started on this journey of teaching literacy to our little loves.

Share Information about Learning Tools

If you have a network of friends who have children, you probably share tips and information with each other. It's fun to chat and share what you've learned about toys and teaching experiences.

Search engines are also helpful, but networking with people adds a special camaraderie and fun to the child-development years when it comes to finding learning tools. Getting together and chatting with friends about good children's books, good children's toys, good children's television shows, and fun places to take children is a part of life that I like to think of as an adventure.

Helpful Tools

There are many places to look for and find the learning tools you enjoy using. The list below includes strong choices to support your child's literacy journey. You'll find these tools are helpful whether this is your first child and you need some beginner's help teaching the ABCs; your children are far apart in age and you're feeling a bit out of the loop with early learning; and even if you already know how to teach the ABCs.

- **Television:** TV offers some very worthwhile kids shows that teach letters, words, colors, and shapes—and also entertain. As an example, today I watched *Daniel Tiger's*

Neighborhood. Daniel's dad took him to the library for story hour. It was a show I'd be happy to have my child watching. *Sesame Street* is another worthwhile children's show. It has been around for years and most kids really enjoy it. There are programs such as *Tumble Leaf* on Prime and *LeapFrog: Letter Factory* on Netflix. Television can provide good back-up support for the teaching we are trying to do in our home. There are many choices.

- **Technology tablets:** Along with broadcast television and streaming services, LeapFrog has educational tools using technology tablets.

- **Online entertainment:** YouTube has a plethora of videos that teach letters in a fun way. One way they do it is by reading popular children's books, such as *The Very Hungry Caterpillar* and *Goodnight Moon* aloud, while showing the illustrations.

- **See-and-hear sound puzzles:** The Melissa and Doug toy company is one of many educational toy companies that make see-and-hear sound puzzles to teach letters and sounds.

- **Older siblings:** Older brothers and sisters are teaching tools too, whether they read to younger children or simply interact with them, showing them more about the world.

- **ABC books and songs:** Alphabet books with beautiful illustrations are helpful. One that I enjoy is Dr. Seuss's *ABC: An Amazing Alphabet Book.* It probably goes without saying that the "ABC song," sung to the melody of "Twinkle, Twinkle Little Star," is almost a must.

- **Magnetic letters:** 3-D magnetic letters that can be arranged and rearranged on a refrigerator door or a whiteboard are fun and useful for many years. These are a great, playful tool for learning letters and spelling out words.

- **Bathtub letters:** Foam letters that stick to tiles and tubs are perfect for bath-time play. I'm sure you can picture kids in the bath singing the "ABC Song" and playing with foam letters while you point them out on the tub walls.

No matter what other tools you use, remember that your best tool is you. Your child's conversations with you about the things they are learning are priceless.

Personalize an ABC Book for Your Child

Another very useful tool is a homemade ABC book. The pictures and topics in the book can be personal to your child, making it a valuable preface to the world of reading.

Marie M. Clay was a distinguished researcher known for her work in educational literacy. It is through her work in Reading Recovery that I became familiar with the idea of a personal ABC book. These books are well worth the time and effort it takes to create them. The process is an enjoyable one-on-one experience that allows input from both you and your child.

How to Create Your Child's Own ABC Book

You'll need a few simple supplies:

- Heavy paper for the book cover

- Fourteen sheets of opaque white paper for the pages. You'll be writing on both sides of each page; choose a heavy-weight paper so the writing doesn't show through.

- A pencil or markers

- Pictures that start with the sound of each corresponding letter. You can use stickers, pictures from magazines, your own photographs, or you can draw your own pictures to correspond with the letters. You don't need to be an artist.

- Scissors

- Glue or paste to attach the pictures to the pages.

- Binding material. You'll need something to bind the book together. You can use a hole punch and secure the pages with yarn or metal paper fasteners, or you can take your finished book to a store like Staples, Office Depot, or Kinkos and have the store assemble it or even laminate it.

The Images You Choose

It's important to use pictures of things that your child recognizes without having to stop and think. Your child should know how to say the name of the image in the picture, as well as knowing what the image represents.

Be sure to avoid confusing images. For example, if you use a picture of a lion for the letter **L**, but your child says "tiger," you need to find another picture. Perhaps you need to use a better-known image for the letter **L**, such as a lamp or a leaf. *Make learning easy and avoid confusion with each letter and picture.*

Putting an ABC Book Together

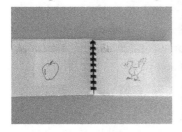 

To assemble the book, use the 14 sheets of white paper. Write the letters of the alphabet in sequential order in the top left corner. Talk about the letters, the names of the letters, and the look of the upper- and lower-case letters.

Now add a picture that starts with each letter. Give your child a choice in the picture selection when you can. For example, ask your child if he would like to use a picture of a **bear** or a **ball** for **Bb**, or a picture of a **zebra** or a **zipper** for **Zz**. In addition to learning the names of the letters, you are helping your child understand the relationship between letters and sounds. When you add a picture to each page, discuss the relationship between the first sound in the word that names the picture and the letter you wrote on the page.

Later in their reading experiences, when children need to remember a sound to get a word started, they can think about their ABC book. The book will help them connect with and recall the sound of a letter, because they know the picture that starts with that letter.

The book will also let you familiarize your child with the use of an apostrophe as a concept to show possession. It will be right there on the cover of their personalized ABC book, in the title that features their name, for example: *John's ABC Book.*

Another bonus for your child's learning is writing "The End" at the back of the book. This gives your child an opportunity to use the short e sound at the beginning of the word **end**. It also allows your child to say the word **the** as **thee**, which is the correct pronunciation when the next word stars with a vowel sound. "The End" also reinforces understanding directional words talked about earlier, in Chapter C.

Remember to take your time with this project. It might take a week. It might take a year. It all depends on when you start, how much time you have, and on your child's readiness. One child might know all their letters at age three, and another child might not learn them until they are five or six. It does not mean that one child is smarter than the other. So, no worries. Take your time and enjoy the journey!

As a side note, in many commercially-published ABC books, I've noticed there is so much "stuff" on every page that it makes it hard to get a child to focus. If you decide to go with an ABC book created by someone other than you and your child, choose a book that isn't too busy with images and other extra material.

It's been my experience that personalized learning plans for children work well. In my opinion, for a strong experience in learning the ABCs, a homemade, personalized ABC book is a winner.

CHAPTER G

Push the "Easy" Button.

"My favorite kind of doughnut is barbarian crème."
—Child, age six

"That was easy!" I have an "easy" button that I bought at an office supply store. It's red, about three inches in diameter, and when you push on it, it says, "That was easy!" I love this button and my students loved it, too. After a reading lesson, they would push it on the way out of the room. It made them smile. It made me smile. And it reminded me of the value of keeping the lesson easy. I didn't want them to think of reading as something that's hard to do.

Whether you are teaching your child letters, words, or story comprehension, keeping it easy is in their best interest. Keep it easy enough to hold their attention and easy enough to avoid struggle and frustration. Of course, the level of "easy" is different for every child, and it changes as you move along with your strategy activities. You have to use your understanding of your child and your instincts to make decisions about the concept of "easy."

Most strategy activities in this book will take about 15 minutes: five minutes to prepare and ten minutes of working together. You can add on an extra minute for hugs. It's a good idea to repeat activities you know your child enjoyed. The main event is having your child's mind working on processing information, finding solutions, and feeling successful and confident. Remember that repetition helps to make things easier when it comes to recognizing letters and words. (It works for grownups too: the more often I make blueberry muffins, the less I have to look at the recipe.)

Gracie in the Library

Gracie in the library is a story that sticks in my memory. Maybe it's better to say this story haunts me. I was walking through the children's section of the library, and as I passed Gracie and her reading tutor, I couldn't help but hear the lesson. I wanted to jump in and save Gracie!

I know Gracie's tutor meant well and really cared about her. The very serious tutor wanted to help, and she was doing what she thought best. But here's what I saw and heard: Gracie was reading a story, word by word, and her tutor was moving a pencil along, under each word, one word at a time. Gracie struggled and frequently needed help with a word. Not surprising: Reading is supposed to sound like talking, not like you're reading a list of words.

As author Lucy McCormick Calkins, the author of *The Art of Teaching Reading* wrote, "A child who has problems with fluency and phrasing often reflects the accumulated experience of reading at frustration level. Our first intervention will be to make certain that this child is on a steady course of books he can read with ease."

I am guessing Gracie was nine or ten years old. I don't know what book they were reading, but I can say for sure *it was too hard*. Reading and practicing reading using easy books would have benefitted Gracie more than struggling in a book that was too hard, reading word by word. It would also have helped this little girl if she used her own finger under the words rather than her tutor guiding her with a pencil. Here are several points that would have helped:

- Remember that reading should sound like talking.

- Choose a book that's easy for your child, no matter what his or her age.

- Encourage your child to point to each of the words they read if they need to. If the book is easy enough, they won't need their finger except at the tricky parts.

Use the Pointer Finger

Many, if not most, emerging readers will use their pointer finger to glide along under the words as they read each sentence. As they learn to make sense of words on a page, the finger directs their focus, helping their eyes and brain work together as they read from left to right and top to bottom. I have also found that this process can be a big help in working with older children who never learned to read properly and are still having problems.

Let me tell you about Jason, a sixth-grade boy, who had a great deal of difficulty reading. I was asked to take a look to see if I could help him. I showed him how words work from left to right and what to do when he is stuck on a word, but the biggest help to him was sliding his finger under the words as he read. Once I had shown him, he could do it on his own to help himself. He could go swiftly from left to right or slowly from left to right. Or he could stop under a word when he was stuck and slide his finger even more slowly as he processed and problem solved.

Another reading expert, Miscese R. Gagen, author of *Right Track Reading Lessons*, discusses the favorable use of finger tracking in her article, "Directional Tracking Explained."

"Start young. You can start teaching this essential skill from the very beginning when you sit your baby or toddler on your lap and read to them. Simply USE YOUR FINGER and follow under the words you are reading. By observing your physical motion, the child learns the essential left-to-right processing of print. Toddlers and preschoolers can even 'help' you read by moving their finger with yours. This is not formal lessons. This is the highly enjoyable snuggling on the couch with your child on your lap reading books together. All you need to add is the simple finger motion and from a very young age the child will acquire this necessary subskill of proficient reading."

"When the child first is learning to read words, require the child to USE THEIR FINGER! This physical motion is highly beneficial in engraining this essential left-to-right processing component of English. The physical pointing motion is also helpful in directing and focusing the child on individual sounds within the word. It helps them 'keep their place' and 'notice all the sounds.' Require physical tracking with the finger until the child has established strong phonologic processing skills, does not make tracking errors, and has learned to pay attention to detail. It is so much more effective and efficient to teach this essential skill correctly from the beginning."

It's Okay

The reason I'm emphasizing the strategy of using your finger to read is because I want everyone to know that it's okay to do. I invited the mother of Jason, the sixth grader I spoke of earlier, to watch a lesson that I was teaching her son. Part of the lesson consisted of reading a book out loud. Jason used his finger and his mom said, "Get your finger out of there." I wasn't expecting that. I wondered if someone had told him to "get his finger out of there" when he was very young and not ready to read without his finger, so he was still struggling to read in sixth grade.

Of course I want children to read with their eyes and not use their finger, but *only when they're ready*. How do you know when children are ready to take their finger away? Begin by asking them to try reading without their finger, and see how it goes. If you're still not sure, try writing short, easy sentences on a piece of paper, one at a time. Ask them to read without a finger. Start with a three-word sentence, then a four-word sentence, then five, and practice.

The Surprise and Delight of Keeping Lessons Easy

I was a Reading Recovery teacher for nine years. Reading Recovery teachers go through intense training to help first-grade children become readers. The student and teacher work together in a one-on-one, 30-minute daily lesson for 20 weeks. By one-on-one, I mean one student with one teacher. One-on-one personal attention is important—and you can do it at home with your child in a time frame that works well with their personality and readiness. And, when you do, keep things easy!

Here is a story about Caleb, a little boy who became a super reader. It was December, almost time for Christmas break. Caleb was in first grade and was still reading from a kindergarten-level book. I was freaking out a little because in my world as a Reading Recovery teacher, I believed that if the child was not improving it was my fault, not his. I still believe that. My tendency was to want to get him into harder books, but I knew better. I stayed the course and did not work with him in books that he was not ready for.

Soon, he was ready for more. Although Caleb was reading at a kindergarten level in December, he was reading at a fourth-grade level in May. Exactly which strategies got the job done remain a mystery. There are so may moving parts in learning to read that it is nearly impossible to pinpoint the tipping point. I can say for sure though, that ease and flow allow success where struggle does not.

Choosing a Just-Right Book

When I attended workshops at Teachers' College at Columbia University in New York, I learned the value of a just-right book. A just-right book is one that your child can pick up and read independently.

What does that mean? It means a book that is easy enough to read, but that still has opportunities for the reader to do a little reading work, like processing through a few words, or rereading a section to get the meaning. Not too easy, not too hard, yet easy enough to enjoy and feel confident about.

And then there is another kind of just-right book—the book that you choose as a teaching book. This will also be easy for your child to read yet it has a few teaching points in it. For example, you may have selected a book that has the word "wanted" used frequently in the story, and you are introducing this word to your child as a word that has two syllables and ends in **-ed**. Your child has the opportunity to read "wanted" again and again within the story.

Here's something to keep in mind when you're working on reading strategies with your child.

Picture a basketball and hoop. You want to position your child close enough to the basket to make the shot. If he is too far from the net and never makes the shot, what fun is it? He quits. In the same way, if he is too close and drops it in every time, what fun is it? He quits. *You want the activity to provide satisfaction in the achievement.*

You know your child best; you can choose just-right activities and adjust the activities to allow learning and success. If you are a sports fan, you may have heard it said that a player is "in the zone." When players are in the zone, they seamlessly perform with excellence. Another way to say it is *in the flow*. When you and your child are in sync during a lesson and moving along with ease, then you are in the zone or in the flow. Those are fun and happy times! Here are some tips for keeping that flow going:

- If you want to pick up speed in reading, read easy books.

- Keep it easy so that when children see a new book, or the magnetic letters, they get excited about learning.

- Create independence by giving more support and avoiding struggle.

Keep the words "ease" and "fun" in mind as you read or do reading work with your child. You know your child best, and you are the creator of the zone for success and successful problem-solving.

CHAPTER H

Help! I'm Stuck.

"Is That Word 'Sent' or 'Nest'?"
—Child, age seven

Sometimes it takes a while to figure out what specific teaching skill you need for helping a child to become a better reader, but when Katie asked me, "Is that word 'sent' or 'nest'?" the answer came to me clear as a bell. The way to help Katie was right there in the problem, but at seven years old, Katie didn't have the strategies to answer that question on her own. Kudos to her though for asking for help. Asking for help is a very good strategy when you don't know what to do. Let's look at how to help Katie help herself the next time she has a problem reading.

How to Help a Child When They Get Stuck on a Word

Good readers know that when we read, our eyes focus from left to right. We don't think about it. It's automatic. But that's not necessarily the case for children learning to read.

Back to Katie: the word she was stuck on was "sent." I asked her if she could get the word started. She wasn't sure what I was asking, so I asked her to put her finger under the first letter.

She did, and she was then able to tell me the correct word. Putting her finger under the first letter was a good strategy to get her eyes to focus where they needed to be. *Calling a child's attention to the first letter is often enough to elicit a correct response. Their answer will help you see what they know and what they need to learn.*

Note: In chapter C, we discussed the importance of making sure your child understands directional words such as **first, next, last, start**, and **end**. You can see why that's important.

Easy-Peasy, but What If . . .

What if Katie didn't know how to start the word, even though I called her attention to the first letter and she put her finger under the correct letter? Keep it easy. I would ask her if she knows another word that starts like that. Maybe she knows the word **stop** or **so** or **sit**, and can think of one of those words to get the sound to start the word **sent**.

More Help on the Way!

If Katie couldn't make the connection between another s-word and **sent** by starting with the same sound, then it would be time to jump in and say, something like "it starts like that word **stop** that you know." By doing that, you not only help her to get a word started, you help her to use something she already knows to help herself; You give her a strategy to problem-solve. *You can do this for your child. Try to use what your child knows to help them figure out something they don't know.*

Using What You Know to Figure Out Something You Don't Know

A little boy named Tyrik really touched my heart. I was working one-on-one with Tyrik, who really wanted to be a good reader. His teacher sent him to me for help. He was already in fifth grade and was a new student in the school.

He began reading a story aloud and when he came to the word **into**, he paused. After doing his best thinking to figure out how to read that word, he read it as **not**. He mustered up all that he knew how to do and gave it a try. He knew the word **not** and was able to find those letters within the word **into**. He dropped the letter **i** because he didn't know what to do with it and rearranged the rest of the letters to read the word **not**.

That's a lot of thinking and brain activity. Wouldn't you agree? After working with him, I understood that he just needed some strategies to put things in order. To help Tyrik, I used easy books, magnetic letters, and one-on-one instruction. I taught him where to start a new word and how to move from left to right within the word to help himself.

Strategies for Your Child to Begin Processing Left to Right

Here are some ways to help a child like Tyrik use left-to-right suggestions and activities to get that process going at an early age. We want a child's brain and eyes to process left to right automatically as they read.

Small Motor Skill Fun

Here's a small motor skill and activity to get the eyes and the hand and the brain all working from left to right in a minute and disciplined way. This is like the left-to-right movement we do when we read words.

- Place different color crayons in a line, I I I I I I, like so. Ask your child to point and name the color. Note: the first few times you do this activity, it's important that the child put their pointer finger underneath each crayon and move from left to right.

- Use the right hand pointer finger, which involves crossing over to start at the left. If you know your child is left handed, use the left-hand pointer finger.

- Rearrange the crayons in a different order and do the exercise again, and again.

After your child has done this a few times, have them name the colors in order without using their finger. If that's difficult, then go back to naming the colors again using the pointer finger.

When I do this activity with children, I frequently change the order of the crayons to add a little more brain work. As always, have fun and praise the good job.

Note: It's always best if you model an activity like this before asking your child to do it. Talk about what you are doing as your child watches.

A Variation on the Crayon Game

Your child probably knows the "ABC song," or at least part of it. If so, do the above activity with magnetic or cutout letters. A B C D E F G.

- Using the pointer finger under the letters, push them up slightly and say or sing the name of the letter.

- Don't mix the order as we did with the crayons.

ILOVEYOU or I LOVE YOU?

This activity will help your child understand the spaces between words. Very young children have no idea that the things we say when we talk are actually separate words. For example, they might think "I Love You," is one word, ILOVEYOU.

- Write each of the words on a separate piece of paper or index card.

- Place them in left-to-right order, I love you.

- Alternatively, write the sentence on a piece of paper, leaving ample space between the words.

- Use your pointer finger under each word as you did with the crayons and the ABCs.

Kicking Things Up a Notch

Here's an activity that's a little more advanced.

- Hold the magnetic letters for the word cat in your closed hands. Shake them like dice. Say, "I have the letters for the word cat in my hands. Let's make the word cat."

- Ask your child to say the word cat very slowly, "like a turtle." Demonstrate saying it slowly, then ask, "When you say the word cat, what sound to you hear first?"

- When they name the first letter, or say the first sound, place the c on the table in front of them. Praise! Awesome! "You heard the first sound! Yay!"

- Now say, "Say the word slowly, like a turtle again, and listen to what sound you hear after the c sound." After you both agree, put the a on the table next to the c.

- Finally say, "Say the word cat slowly like a turtle one more time and tell me what you hear after the a." Put the t on the table.

- Check the word cat by running your finger carefully under the word, listening to the sounds coming out of your mouth, matching the letters.

You can do this activity with other words too. Choices might include: **big, mom, did, red, cup, dad, stop,** to name a few. Each of these words contains one of the five short vowel sounds for **a, e, i, o, u.**

- Practice saying words slowly and a bit sing-songy: c-aaaat, b-iiiig, m-ooooom.

- Emphasize the first sound. Sound the following letters a bit more softly, and slowly, like a turtle, listening for the letter sounds and their order.

Note: This technique will come in handy in later school years. It's a tool for spelling words correctly on spelling tests.

The Slide, a Self-Check Strategy

Show your child how to slide their pointer finger from left to right under a word to check the sound of the word and how the different sounds match the letters.

- Here are a few words for this activity: **cat, am, mom, yes, not, and, pig, red, hat**. You can make the words with magnetic letters or write them on a sheet of paper or a whiteboard.

- Work on one word at time. Practice this activity with words your child already knows so they learn the strategy and can then apply it to a new word when and if it's needed.

Left Page Before Right Page

It's easy but important to talk to children about reading the left page before the right page. When they open a book, small children may read or look at the picture on the righthand side, then turn the page and only look at the righthand page again—and again. It takes only a little conversation with your child to start them reading or looking at the left page first. It's easy to do.

Sight Words to Memorize

I was stunned when a colleague told me her son had to know 100 sight words in kindergarten. Sight words are words that appear frequently in reading, words like: **the, and, like, I, see, go,** and **will.**

There are two ways for a child to learn to recognize 100 words. One is to memorize them and the other is to know how to get a word started and move from left to right sounding and processing. Good readers use both techniques.

So why was I stunned? First, 100 is a lot of words. Second, because I know how families are affected by such requirements: They're easy for some families and stressful or maybe even impossible for others. And thirdly because I'd rather a child be learning words through stories rather than memorizing lists.

That said, however, memorizing sight words does help, especially with words that are odd or that don't totally match the sounds coming out of our mouths as we speak: words such as **could, night, pretty, some, where, said, who, again, walk, eat, what, was,** and **saw.** These are all frequently used words, and a reader's life is easier if they know them on sight.

Samantha's Problem Was Not Immediately Obvious

I was tutoring seven-year-old Samantha, who had an excellent command of language. It was easy to see that she was very intelligent, so why was she having difficulty reading? Why was she being pulled out of class for special reading help in a small group?

Samantha began reading an easy book out loud. Her verbal expression was amazing, as if she was telling a story. And then it happened. She paused. I waited, giving her think-time. It turned out that she was contemplating the word **help**. She said **play**. She looked at me to see what I thought of her guess. I asked her to get the word started. She couldn't. She didn't know the sound of **h**, and she responded as she did because she didn't know how to help herself. By asking her to get the word started, I learned how to help her. Once she knew the sound of **h**, she was on her way.

Katie, who we met earlier on page 61, couldn't read the word **sent** because she didn't know that she should start with the first letter when she was stuck. Samantha couldn't read the word help because she didn't know the sound of h. "Can you get that word started?" just might be the single most important question to ask your child if they get stuck! If they can't get it started, find out why. It could change your child's life!

Tips to Remember

- Say words very slowly, "like a turtle." Children love animals and will probably think it's fun to talk like a turtle.

- Use short words like, **mom, dad, cat, am, big, red,** and **run**. The sounds in these words are easy to hear.

- Say the word like a turtle yourself, then ask your child to say it like a turtle.

- Emphasize the first-letter sound and then gently and slowly sound the rest of the word. The point of saying words this slowly is so that children notice the sounds coming out of their mouth. They hear the sounds coming out of your mouth and then hear and feel the sounds coming out of their mouth.

- Smooth the sounds together. For example, for **mom**, say mmmoooommm, slowly like a turtle, almost as if you are humming the word **mom**.

Having proper tools makes any job easier and giving your child the understanding of how words work is a tool that will make their job as a reader easier. By teaching and learning about words, you will give your child problem-solving skills, ways to think and help themselves.

CHAPTER I

Praise Your Child . . . or Shoot Yourself in the Foot.

"As soon as I'm done growing, I'm out of here!
I'll be 20 or 25 by then."
—Child, age six

"Mom . . . Mom . . . Mom . . . Mom!"

"Will you please answer him?"

My sister and I were chatting over a cup of coffee. One of my three little children wanted to get my attention. He wasn't going to give up. I didn't pay attention and my sister finally intervened on his behalf and said, "Will you please answer him."

Children want our attention. And when they have it, it's important that we look for the good. The same is true when it comes to reading; it's important that we give our attention to the good that children do in their journey toward learning to read.

The Definition of Praise: Express Warm Approval or Admiration

When your baby took a first step at 11 or 12 months, I'm pretty sure you clapped and shouted, "Yay!" No doubt you shouted encouraging sounds before your little one actually took that step. This positive attention was of great value both to you and your child.

Do you remember that happy, excited feeling? Your child loved getting the positive attention and you loved giving it. I want to encourage you to continue taking the path of positive attention and words of praise for your wonderful and deserving child. Praise is a way of guiding your child's focus. It's not manipulation, it's positive guidance and a very pleasant way of expressing what it is you would like your child to repeat.

Keep an eye out for things children do right rather than what they do wrong, then praise the behavior. This is especially true when children are learning to read!

Sample Praises

Good job putting your toothbrush back in the holder.

I like the way you helped your brother pick up his toys.

You are so good at chewing with your mouth closed.

You are so good at playing by yourself for a little while.

You're such a good thinker. Thanks for the good idea.

You are such a good listener.

I love reading to you and listening to what you have to say about the story.

This is a really good book that you chose.

> Thank you for helping me hold the book.
>
> I like how you got that word started.
>
> I like how you got the word started and checked the picture to help yourself read that tricky word.

Children learn behaviors through observation, by being taught, and through personal experience—among other avenues. We can solidify what behaviors are beneficial to them by guiding their attention and focusing on those positive behaviors through praise.

Modeling to Make a Difference

When we praise, we are modeling the concept of *looking for the good*. Wouldn't it be wonderful if your child was inspired by your praise and looked for the good in others?

It was through the teaching of reading that I learned the value of praise and looking for the good. As we guide a child's thinking through clear instruction and praise, we have the opportunity to model thought patterns that children can use to solve their own reading problems This skill can translate to solving problems of all kinds.

One of my favorite questions, and one that I want children to ask is, "What can I do to help myself?" It has been an amazing experience each time I've seen children solve their own reading problems. Their eyes light up like the lights on a Christmas tree. They feel so proud. They look at me and I say, "Yay! I like the way you helped yourself!"

It's beyond exciting when children use the same praise on another child. They're paying it forward, using the behavior you modeled. When a big brother says to his little brother, "Good job!" or, "It was cool the way you figured it out," you know you've succeeded in getting the idea across.

In my experience, praise really supports reading. You won't find this in a textbook on the subject, but teaching has shown me the value of praise through the results I get from young readers. Our minds work in interesting ways, and praising good reading behaviors encourages children to read.

The Key to Many Things

In fact, praise encourages children to learn to solve problems of all kinds. It can help children have fun and to believe in themselves—which in turn encourages their joy in learning. I've seen what looking for the good and praising the good can do. It's not unrealistic to suggest that the habit of praise could be part of the solution to a wide variety of things in your child's life.

What Kind of Praise Is Best?

Clear, specific praise is usually best. General praise is better than no praise, but when you're clear and specific, it's more believable; it focuses on the behaviors we would like a child to remember and repeat. For instance, telling a child, "I love the way you drew all those little details in your picture. You're really good at noticing things," is better than just saying, "That's a nice picture."

Praise Specific to Learning to Read

Let's look at how praise supports and guides your young student on the journey toward learning to read, using a five-minute mini lesson.

You: "Timmy, I'm going to say the word **am**, slowly like a turtle."

[Make the short **a** sound and then the m sound—aaaaaaa mmmmmmm.]

Now, you say it, slowly like a turtle.

[Smile and give your child think time.]

Timmy: "Aaaaaaa mmmmmmmm."

You: "Wow! That was soooo good. Let's do that again. Aaaaaaa mmmmmmm. Your turn, Timmy. "

Timmy: "Aaaaaaa mmmmmm."

You: "Great job! Now, I'm going to give you the letter **a** to put on the table as you make the **a** sound. I'll show you."

[You are modeling. You place the **a** on the table and say aaaaaaaa. Give the **a** to Timmy.]

Timmy: [Puts the **a** on the table and makes the **a** sound.] "Aaaaaaa."

You: "Yay! And now I'm going to give you the letter **m** to put next to the **a.** I'll show you." [Place the **m** next to the **a.**] Mmmmmm. [Give the **m** to Timmy.]

Timmy: [Puts the **m** next to the **a.**] "Mmmmm."

You: "Timmy, you just made the word **am**!"

[Slide your finger carefully under the word and say **am.** Now ask Timmy to slide his finger under the word.]

You: "Look how smart you are, Timmy!"

Play a game and show Timmy how to shake the letters in his closed hands, like dice. Ask him to make the word **am** on the table. Check the word and ask him to check. If he gets it right, check it for him by sliding your finger under the word. Ask him to check it. Now it's time to praise with words or a high five or a fist bump!

What if he gets it wrong? If he gets it wrong, don't forget to praise him for trying. Let's say he puts the **m** first and then the **a**. Praise him anyway! Say, "Good job putting the letters next to each other." Then say, "Let's put the a first because the aaaaaa sound comes out of our mouth first."

Another way you might praise his effort would be to say, "You did a good job shaking the letters." Sometimes we have to get creative with the praise.

That was a lesson that took approximately five minutes. You had an opportunity to spend time together, to offer praise, and to learn a little about what your child is ready to learn. Some children need a little more think time before they answer a question. That's just fine, just say,

"I like the way you were thinking about the question and the answer."

Staying in the Zone

One of the important things I've learned from attending conferences and reading books and from personal experience with children is *the teacher creates the zone for learning*. If we make a lesson too hard, the child's learning system shuts down. (Think of it as a trapdoor that connects the brain stem to the brain slamming shut.) It's a reaction caused by anxiety or fear.

It's best to keep things easy and positive so that learning can occur. *We can introduce and teach new information as long as we present it in a way that does not create stress*. I find that I am more patient when I keep lessons easy and stress free. I admit that it can be tricky to move forward with new information and keep things easy at the same time, but striking a balance between the two is important.

Replace "But" with "And"

"That was a delicious dinner, but…" When my husband says that, I'm pretty sure my heart shuts down for a second. Or how about this one, "I really like that outfit you're wearing, but…"

The word "but" after a compliment is so deflating. During a mini lesson, or when you are complimenting or praising children for something they say or do, try replacing the word "but" with the word "and."

Instead of saying, "I like that you ran your finger under the word to check if the letters match the sounds coming out of your mouth, **but** you went too fast and your finger went way past the last letter," say, "I like that you ran your finger under the word to check if the letters match the sounds coming out of your mouth, **and** I like it when you go slow and do it like this." Then, be sure to model slow and careful checking.

Here's another example, "Thanks for taking out the garbage, **but** you didn't close the back door." Instead, you could say: "Thanks for taking out the garbage, and please close the back door."

You get the idea. We don't want to cause anxiety with our words or with our attitude, especially when we are helping a child learn.

The Five Love Languages of Children

I recently read *The Five Love Languages of Children*, by Gary D. Chapman and Ross Campbell, and I am so excited about this book. I hope every parent reads it. It applies to children from birth to 18, and the premise is that all children have a "love tank" that needs to be filled. Children are happier when their love tank is full, and we all want our children to be happy. The authors discuss "Five Love Languages" that are needed to keep that tank full: Words of Affirmation, Acts of Service, Gifts, Quality Time, and Physical Touch. Very young children need all five.

"If your child is under age four, speak all five languages. Tender touch, supporting words, quality time, gifts, and acts of service all converge to meet your child's need for love. If that need is met and your child genuinely feels loved, it will be far easier for him to learn and respond in other areas."

How Can We Use the Love Languages with Reading?

Physical Touch: A hug! Read a story together with your child on your lap.

Words of Affirmation: Remember to say, "Good job! I like the way you checked the picture to help you understand the story."

Quality Time: Take the time to read together or to do a reading strategy together.

Gifts: Wrap a new book that you will enjoy together in gift paper.

Acts of Service: Help children with material they are trying to understand by creating flash cards or prompts on Post-it notes.

It's much easier to teach your child to read or to get ready to read if their love tank is full. In fact, I'm thinking if their love tank is full, life with your child will be easier and fuller in many ways. Remember: Everyone deserves to feel loved.

Expect Smiles, Fist Bumps, High Fives, and Fun!

You'll see more smiles and have more fun when you give attention with praise. I don't believe in constructive criticism. Honestly, criticism is shooting yourself in the foot, and you don't have to take my word for it. Find out for yourself! Look for reasons to praise your child and have fun.

Think and Link
with Color Words

"I have to wear glasses because I have
a torn red nut in my eye."
—Child, age six

Red **Yellow** **Green** **Blue** **Black** **Brown** **Purple**

Children start learning their colors around the age of two. By the age of four or five they've got it down—they know their colors and they likely learned them from you. We are going to kick things up a notch; learning color words can be helpful when learning how to read other words.

I want to be clear that the appropriate age for any learning activity depends on the child. You know your child best. You can tell if they're ready to learn something new by their interest and their attitude. Learning is easier when we can connect something new to something we already know. *Children who know their color words have a powerful tool to help them read new words.*

Knowing the color words as sight words—looking at the word and knowing how to read it just by sight—is a good start. Knowing the pieces that go together to make the color words is even better. Children can use what they know to learn more.

Let's assume you've taught the color words and your child can read them on flashcards and make them with magnetic letters and maybe even write them. Let's see how useful these words can be for a beginning reader.

red

- If your child is reading and comes to a word he doesn't know and it starts with the letter r you can say, "That word starts like the word **red** that you know."

- Be careful with the sound of the **r**. Many people say **er** (as in her) for the **r** sound. When sounding the r, you have a small opening in your mouth and you feel the little motor-like sound coming out slowly and carefully.

- Some words have the **ed** sound at the end, like the **ed** in red. If you come to the word **wanted** in a story, you can do a little teaching by saying, "Can you hear the way the word **wanted** sounds at the end? It sounds like the **ed** at the end of the word **red**." More words where you can use this tool are: **fed, bed, needed, decided**.

- If your child is ready to learn the short vowel sounds, you can say, "That's a short e. It sounds like the **e** you hear in the middle of **red**." Some words where you might use this tool are: **end, else, exit, ten, hen, send**.

- Be sure to give some "wait time" for the answer.

yellow

I have seen children struggle with learning the sound of **y**. If they know **yellow**, you can say, "You know the sound of **y**. It's the sound you hear at the start of **yellow**."

- To read or learn new words like, **well, tell, sell,** or **fell**, you can say, "Get the word started and then it's got the **ell** part like in **yellow**."

green
- The word **green** has the **gr** like in **grandpa** and **grass** and **grumpy**. If your child is trying to read a word that starts with **gr** and looks at you for assistance, you can say, "That word starts like **green**. Can you start that word?"

- The **ee** in **green** is found in many other words that appear in children's books. Of course, it's not to be confused with the **e** in **red**. You can say, "**ee** sounds like the middle of **green**," to help with words like **feed, keep, bee, and jeep.**

- Remember, give your child some "wait time" for coming up with the answer.

blue, black, brown
- There is magic in these three words! They all start with the letter **b**. Some children confuse **b** and **d**. I have seen children confuse b and d as late as fourth grade. It's best to have a clear understanding at an early age.

- If your child pauses when they get to a word that starts with **b**, you can say, "That word starts like those color words you know."

- If your child pauses at a word that starts with a **d**, you can say, "Think about those color words you know. Does that start like **blue**?" If they aren't sure, write the word

blue and talk about the difference between **b** and **d**. Remind your little one to think about what they already know, like the word, **blue**, so they can help themselves when stuck.

- You can simply tell a child the word they're stuck on, but try to make a learning connection. If the word is **baby**, for example, you can say, "That word is **baby**. It starts like the word **blue** that you know." Give the word and make a connection.

- Give your child some wait time for the answer.

purple
- The word **purple** has amazing value. If your child gets stuck on a work that starts with a **p**, like **pig** or **puppy** or **pancake**, you can say, "It starts like that word **purple** that you know." You can also give the new word and say, "That word is **pig**. It starts like that word **purple** that you know."

- Purple has an **le** at the end, as do many other words, such as **apple, little, table**.

- The **le** is a unique little piece that you can use to help explain the silent e by saying, "That's the word **apple**. It ends like the word **purple** that you know. The e is on the end to make the word look right."

- Purple has a **ur** piece that can help with words like **hurt, purr, fur, turn**. If a child can get the word **turn** started because they know **t**, and then looks at you for help, you can say, "That has the **ur** like in the word **purple**. It says **ur** and the word is **turn**."

- Allow your child some wait time for the answer.

Remember to use word pieces, or chunks, such as the **ack** in **black** or the **ur** in **purple**, because as you move forward in helping your child learn to read, you'll find that sounding one letter at a time is not necessary if they know and understand pieces of words that are used in many words.

Word Pieces

If you want to teach pieces of words, or chunks, that come *after* the first letter, here are a few samples using **ack, ue, own**, that are grouped together here with rhyming words.

bl**ack**	bl**ue**	br**own**
s**ack**	d**ue**	cl**own**
t**ack**	cl**ue**	d**own**
J**ack**	gl**ue**	
p**ack**		

Exactly what is wait time?

Picture a six-year old looking up at you with a look in their eyes that seems to say, "Why did you tell me the answer? I knew that." I have had that experience.

I've learned from children that we have to give them a chance to think when we ask a question, especially a question that is asking them to link what they know to what is new. Often, I would say, "Do you want me to tell you or do you need more time to think?" Sometimes children have wanted me to tell them and sometimes they wanted to think and give it a try.

Although I've given you examples of how to guide children's thinking to figure out a new word, there is no need to use my exact words for this process. Change it up to fit the situation.

Seriously, This Can Be Fun

Have fun teaching color words. For instance, you can have Red Week at your house. Your child can:

- Wear a red shirt.

- Use a red crayon for coloring or drawing.

- Use magnetic letters to make the word red.

- Use a red marker to write on the whiteboard.

- Make red food, like Jell-O or jelly or pizza.

- Write the word **red** on flashcards and put them all around the house.

- Read *Clifford the Big Red Dog* by Norman Bridwell. Show your child the word red in the title and the word **red** in the story. Read it again the next day, and ask your child to find and point out the word **red**. Have fun!

Choose activities like these, and repeat them for each color. Of course, you can add to the list with your own ideas, and feel free to take longer than a week for each color if that works better for your child. By calling your child's attention to color words in a book, you'll help them see that words are part of stories.

Books for Yellow, Blue, Black, Purple, and Many Other Colors

Here is a list of books using color words. Each of these books is popular and you can find them at the library as well as online.

- *Brown Bear, Brown Bear, What Do You See?* By Eric Carle

- *Harold and the Purple Crayon*, by Crockett Johnson

- *Baa, Baa Black Sheep*, nursery rhyme (can be sung to the tune of the "ABC song.")

- *Green Eggs and Ham*, by Dr. Seuss

- *The Artist Who Painted the Blue Horse,* by Eric Carle

- *The Rainbow Fish*, by Marcus Pfister

Flashcards and Legos

Flashcards and Legos are both terrific tools for helping children learn to read using color words.

Flashcards are inexpensive, versatile, and hands-on. You can make your own by using simple index cards. Using the colors of Legos to match with the words on flashcards is a natural pairing.

- Write a color word on each flashcard.

- Place Legos in a row and put the flashcard with the corresponding color word in front of each.

Or, do this as a sorting activity.

- Give your child a pile of Legos to sort into piles of red, yellow, green, blue, black, brown, and purple.

- Ask your child to put the flashcard with the color word on it in front of the correct pile.

Note: Depending on your child's age, you might want to model the entire activity first.

In the End, You're the Boss, You Choose

Using color words for activities is just one tool for you to use with your child. You can use other sets of words with these activities as well. Perhaps you will decide to use animal words, such as **dog, cat, pig, mouse**, or **rabbit** instead of, or in addition to, color words. Adapt the activity to the words.

For example, make flash cards with the animal words. Make the word **dog** with magnetic letters. Locate the word dog in books. Now you can link new words to the animal words just as you can link new words to known color words. Try it with easy action words like, **skip, run, jump, walk,** and **hop**. The action words become the known words. Teach your child to link new words to the known action words. You know your child best. You know what they are ready for and when they are ready.

Conversations about words and stories and how they go together are key to helping your child understand how written language works. This type of conversation will help your child figure out the solutions for reading words they don't immediately recognize.

Short conversations about a specific way to think, and pointing out something for your child to notice, will go a long way toward raising a reader. As always, the bottom line is, have fun and look for things to praise!

CHAPTER K

My Child Can Read . . . Sort Of

"When the vowel breaks the cradle will fall."
—Child, age six

Have you ever been snow skiing? The Level 1 ski slope is the bunny hill. That's where you learn how to fall and get back up, many times. Next is Level 2. That's where you practice staying up on your skis and learning to stop. I was pretty excited when I got there, and I moved myself on to Level 3. The ski patrol saw me. He skied over and politely told me to go back to Level 2. It was obvious I was not ready for Level 3. (Just a little embarrassing!)

There Is No Reading Patrol

If a child is given a book, how do we know if it is too hard? *We* are the reading patrol. So, what should we do? I don't want you to go to a parent-teacher conference one day and hear that, "Your child can read, but he doesn't comprehend what he is reading." Or, "Your child can read but he's levels behind where he should be."

How Can We Tell If a Book Is "Just Right" for a Reader?

Lucy McCormick Calkins, author of *The Art of Teaching Reading*, gives us a good idea of a "just-right" book. "First and most important, we notice if children are reading with engagement and responsiveness. If a child laughs at the funny parts, or brings the book to recess in order to continue reading, we have a pretty good indication that this is a just-right book. But I also recommend asking a child to read out loud and listening to the child's phrasing and fluency. Does this *sound* like language?"

Leveled Books

Some schools use leveled books. This means that each child is reading at a level that is just right for them. The levels are usually referred to as Level A, Level B, Level C, and on to Level Z.

The intention is for books to be the appropriate reading level and the appropriate subject matter for each student. There is more than one leveling system. Some leveling systems use numbers instead of letters. You will want to check with your child's school for information on their reading program. They may give you a chart or list of the levels for each grade.

Reading Level Samples

Let's look at some sample pages of reading levels progressing from easy to more difficult. The first example is a kindergarten level and the last example is an end-of-first-grade level.

If we are raising a reader it is good to have an understanding of where they're headed. I'm not labeling all the levels shown below, because I mainly want to give you an idea of how reading levels progress in difficulty. All of these levels would be matched with illustrations to help with meaning.

I see the bus.

Look at Mom.

Mom is in the yard.

"I like to run," said the boy.

I can see the dog and the cat.

They are playing with the ball.

The deer ran into the woods.

He ran fast.

"Where is he going?' shouted Sam.

My dog is under the bed.

She is looking for the ball. It is not there.

"I want to catch a fish.

Is this a good day to fish?" said Fred.

"This is a good day to fish," said Dad.

The squirrel ran around the yard and over the fence.

Once upon a time, a king couldn't find his crown.

He looked and looked.

It was under the big chair.

I wanted to play outside, but after the rain, the yard was too muddy. So, I played inside.

Mike and Jill went swimming.

"We love to swim," they said, "and the water isn't too cold."

> The big hungry dog walked over to his bowl of food. He ate the food and then he slurped some water. SLURP! Next, he walked over to the door and barked. RUFF! RUFF!
> His master opened the door and out he went.

It's Not Always Easy to Know

It's not always easy to know which book level is best for your child at any given time.

Each level has books that are easy reading and hard reading within it. It's not an exact science, but using leveled books helps us guide little readers on their paths to becoming successful, independent readers. The best level for a child at any point along this path, however, is the level at which a child can read without struggle, sounding like a reader, almost sounding like normal conversation as they read aloud.

It's important to master one level before moving on to the next. Some children stay at the beginning levels longer than others. No worries. *Staying at the right level when they are first learning is what will eventually allow a child to move on to higher levels faster and more easily.* A child might need to read five or ten books at the same level before mastering the level and moving on to the next. That's just fine!

A Few Things to Keep in Mind

Keeping in mind that children mature at their own pace, physically and mentally, it's our job to support them where they are in their growth. We wouldn't disapprove if our child is not at a certain height at age six, and we shouldn't disapprove if our child is not at a certain reading level at age six.

When teaching a larger group of children, I keep in mind that they are of varied ages. If a kindergarten's cut-off for birth dates is August 10, that means there could be a child who turned five on August 10 in the class along with a child who turned six on August 11. That second child missed the cut-off date by one day and now is a whole year older than the child who just squeaked in under the date. This is one more reason to support a child where their abilities are at any given time. It's nothing to worry about, just something to be aware of when you compare one child to another.

Who's Ready for Second Grade?

Something important that I have noticed in my years of working with young readers is that second grade is where struggle starts to show itself. And it gets louder and clearer as the year moves along.

Many of the students I have been asked to tutor were in second grade. Sometimes I was asked to tutor a third-grade student, and the situation was the same, it just took teachers a year longer before reaching for help. It is my professional opinion that these children were moved to a higher level before mastering a lower level. They were moved along even though they were struggling with grade-level expectancies.

When I was successful in helping a child get to where they needed to be, it was by having the child read at their level—or even easier levels—until they sounded like a reader and had the confidence of a reader. Then we proceeded to move up a level. Reading lots and lots of easy and at-level texts can have amazing results. Although sometimes it takes only one book at a level, other times it takes ten books or more at that level before moving up. It's the process for reading success.

There can be a variety of reasons why a child misses the important steps in one reading level before moving ahead. Among them are:

- Absence from school due to an illness

- Upcoming holidays or birthday that distract a child's concentration in class

- Lack of sleep

- Hunger

- Mom is having a baby

All children want to learn. It's up to us to be sensitive to their individual personalities and abilities.

What a Nice Surprise

A friend of mine took her child to school for kindergarten testing. The teacher and child sat next to each other. The teacher asked questions and, as the boy answered, she wrote down the answers. That's how testing is done. Well, my friend's son suddenly gave an answer before the teacher asked the question. There was a pause. Then she said, "How did you know that? Looking down at her paper, he said, "Well, it says it right there." He could read!

That boy has two older sisters who loved to read. Did he learn from watching them and listening to their conversations? Did he learn from television shows that are part-cartoon and part-teaching in nature? His mom didn't know he could read. It was a nice surprise.

On the Other Side of the Coin

A former coworker called me and asked what she could do to help an eighth-grade boy. He was a struggling reader. After some testing, we agreed to begin with end-of-first-grade reading material, because that is where he could read comfortably, sounding like a reader, and that is what worked. We were sensitive to his situation and we gave him material that he could take home to practice reading aloud. It was tricky getting the material to him and not letting his peers in on it.

Playing catch-up is difficult, because as children get older they have many interests and learning to be a better reader is not necessarily one of them, especially if reading is difficult.

The teacher is guiding this boy and, most importantly, giving him at-level reading material. Children can move up very quickly once they spend the right amount of reading time at their level. I'm confident this boy will improve.

Reading List

The following is a list of books that are available on Amazon, at the library, and in bookstores. I've arranged them by level, from kindergarten through the end of first grade.

You want your child to read out loud while both of you are looking at the book and the words. Remember to keep it easy and to give support and praise. *You are not testing your child, you are acquiring an understanding of what your child knows how to do.*

A *One Hunter*, by Pat Hutchins

B *Dressing Up*, Rigby PM Platinum Collection

C *All Fall Down*, by Helen Oxenbury

D *Fishing*, Rigby PM Platinum Collection

E *Have You Seen My Cat*, by Eric Carle

F *Bears on Wheels*, by Stan and Jan Berenstain

G *Flying*, by Donald Crews

H *Five Little Monkeys Jumping on the Bed*, by Eileen Christelow

H *All By Myself*, by Mercer Mayer

I *Just Like Daddy*, by Frank Asch

J *Cars,* by Anne Rockwell

K *Dinosaurs, Dinosaurs,* by Byron Barton

K *Just for You,* by Mercer Mayer

L *Biscuit,* by Alyssa Capucilli

L *Titch,* by Pat Hutchins

M *Old Hat New Hat,* by Stan and Jan Berenstain

N *You'll Soon Grow into Them, Titch,* by Pat Hutchins

N *There Was an Old Lady Who Swallowed a Fly,* by Pam Adams

O *Are You My Mother?* by P. D. Eastman

O *The Napping House,* by Don and Audrey Wood

P *Happy Birthday, Sam,* by Pat Hutchins

Q *Where the Wild Things Are,* by Maurice Sendak

R *The Cat in the Hat,* by Dr. Seuss

R *If You Give a Mouse a Cookie,* by L. J. Numeroff

S *Frog and Toad Are Friends,* by Arnold Lobel

Saving the Best for Last

Comprehension. It's a big deal. You can't become engaged in a story if you're not comprehending the message. Agreed? Here are some ways to improve comprehension:

Use the illustrations: Use a book's pictures to support understanding. The pictures in children's books almost tell the story without words. Talk about the pictures before you read a book to your child or before they read a book to you—when you feel it would be beneficial. Let the pictures help carry the meaning.

Talk about storytelling: Stories have a beginning, middle, and end. To give children a first-hand understanding of how stories progress in books, ask them to tell you a real-life story. For example, if your child goes to the movies with Nana, ask about it when they get home.

- Where did you go?

- What did you do first?

- Then what did you do?

- What did you do next?

- How did the day with Nana end?

Through conversation, help your child connect real life to life in a book. Remember, stories in real life have a beginning, middle, and end too.

One Last Comprehension Tip

When children are reading aloud, try to notice whether or not they are listening to themselves. Sometimes children sound amazing when they read to us. They are proud of themselves and they want us to be happy and proud of them. Nudge them to listen to what they are reading. Simply ask, "Are you listening to yourself when you read?" I witnessed a student experience a huge jump in his reading ability after I asked him that question and he started listening!

You Are on the Runway

There are many variables on the path to learning to read. Some children can read all the words with ease and yet do not understand what they just read. On the other hand, some children comprehend what is being read to them, but they struggle with reading words themselves. I have confidence that you will guide your little reader.

You are on the runway together. It's exciting that, one day, your child will take off and become an independent reader. Enjoy your time together and have fun!

Let the Magnetic Letters Do Their Magic

"Where is the magnet tying glass?"
Child—age six

I just had to title this chapter **LMNOP**! When we sing the "ABC song," we smoosh those five letters together. What's a child to think? What is an elemenopee?

With that in mind, here are some activities to do with children to help them have a clearer understanding of letters and how to think about them.

Three Ways to Learn New Information

I like to give children ways to see, hear, and do things when they are learning. The different learning styles are defined in this description from "Your Dictionary," online.[3]

"The way people learn and process new information that they are taught is one of the many factors that makes each individual person unique. While some people learn quickly by actually performing a task for themselves, others learn better by watching someone do the task or by simply hearing the task explained. The method that each person prefers for learning is known as their own unique learning style. For teachers and parents, understanding your child's learning style can be the key to unlocking their full potential and making difficult concepts seem easy as can be."

So, how to provide those three experiences?

Using magnetic letters allows for all three: see, hear, and do. My favorite brand of magnetic letters is Quercetti. The letters are made of hard plastic. They are very colorful and just right for children's little hands. Note that the packaging for these letters states that they are for ages three and up, and I assume that is because some children put things in their mouths. You know best on that matter.

Use lowercase magnetic letters for most of the following activities. I ordered one set of uppercase and two sets of lowercase, which might be a good idea for you, too.

Let's get started.

Activity # 1 Loving the "ABC Song"
A task for children to see, hear, and do

At some point in your child's early years, I'm pretty sure you will be singing the "ABC song" together. Here's an activity to help children understand what they are singing.

 I use a steel cookie sheet and line up the letters in order. The magnetic letters stick to the sheet. Show you child how to put their pointer finger under each letter as you sing. This is simple, valuable, clear, and precise teaching. First you do it, then they do it. Do this as many times as it takes until it is easy—and have fun!

To be most effective, make sure your child's finger is *under* each letter, so that they can clearly see the letter when it is named. If they put their finger on the letters, it will block a clear view.

Activity #2 Sort by Color
A task for children to see and do

The easiest activity is to sort the letters by color. Simply make piles: a yellow pile, a blue pile, an orange pile, a green pile, and a red pile.

Model the activity first and then do it together. Then when children are confident, they can do it alone. You can do this with or without the cookie sheet.

Activity #3 Sort by Short Sticks and Long Sticks
A task for children to see and do

Put these nine letters into a bowl or on the cookie sheet, **b, h, k, l, t,** *a*, **m, n, r, u.** Show your child how to sort the letters into two groups. One group will have letters with long sticks and one group will have letters with short sticks.

Next, you can kick it up a notch, and name the letters and their sounds. Notice that the **n** could be an upside-down **u**.

Shake it all up and do it again. Have fun!

Activity #4 Make Your Name
A task for children to see, hear, and do

Using magnetic letters, show your child how to make their name. Talk about it. Talk about how it starts with a capital letter, how many letters are in the name, and what a wonderful name it is!

If you think your child can do this alone, mix up the letters and ask if they want to try it. Notice and compliment whatever part they get right. If they're not ready to do it alone, you can say something like, "Watch me. I'll do it again for you. Let me see. First, I'll put the capital letter, **M**. Hmmm, next I'll put the little **a**. Now I'll put the letter t and the last letter **t**. **Matt**!"

If your child's name has one syllable, like **Tim**, **Jen**, or **Pam**, this will be pretty easy. If your child's name has two syllables, like **Jackson**, first teach **Jack**, and make **Jack** with magnetic letters, then teach **son** with magnetic letters, then put it together.

If your child's name is **Romeo**, first teach **Ro**, then **me**, then **o**. Put it all together and it says **Romeo**. If your child's name is **Zoe**, first teach **Zo**, then **e**. Put it together and it says **Zoe**.

Breaking words into syllables is what we do when we write, so breaking words into syllables with magnetic letters is a healthy early start to writing, spelling, and reading new words.

It's my experience that children love to shake the letters in their hands, just like dice, and then do the activity. When you are sure an activity is easy for your child, you can make it even more fun by shaking the letters and saying, "Can you make the name fast?" Fast is fun. As always, be sure to have fun and offer praise!

Activity #5 Another Way to Make Your Name
A task for children to see and do

For this activity, start by writing your child's name, large and clear, on a piece of paper.

Then, place the corresponding magnetic letters below each of the letters you've just written.

Starting at the left, ask your child to name each letter. As they do, move the magnetic letter up to cover the written letter. This is helpful if your child has a long or difficult name.

Activity #6 Match Uppercase Letters with Lowercase Letters
A task for children to see and do

"Uppercase **A**" is another way of saying "capital **A**" or "big **A**." "Lowercase a" is another way of saying "little **a**." I'm going to refer to letter forms as "capital" and "little."

This activity is about matching capital letters with their little letter partner. Start with five capital letters and their partners.

Talk about capital letters and little letters. You might want to show how these letters look in a book. Books mainly have little letters but some words start with a capital letter.

Next—using either just a few select letters or all 26—put the capital letters into one group and the little letters in another. You can use the cookie sheet for this or just set the letters on the table.

Show your child how to take a capital letter and find its little partner and put them together, such as **Aa, Cc, Ee, Ff, Mm.**

Writing Goes from Sound to Letter, Reading from Letter to Sound

Having taught hundreds of children to read, I've met children who could write the word they were saying or thinking but could not read back the story they wrote. In this case, they were going from sound to letter successfully, but they were unable to go from letter to sound.

Reading and writing are two sides of a coin. It's in your child's interest to learn to use their skills effectively to both read and write with ease. One of the best ways to do this is to help them look at a letter and make the sound of that letter—and then do the opposite: make a sound and identify the letter it belongs to. Here are two activities you can use to nurture these skills:

Activity #7 Going from Sound to Letter
A task for children to see, hear, and do

Start by choosing a two- or three-letter word. For example: **mom, dad, me, cat, so, go, at, can, run, dog**. Say it out loud. For example, say the word **can**, emphasizing the first sound.

With the set of magnetic letters ready, ask, "What sound do you hear at the beginning of **can**? What letter should I give you to start the word **can**?"

If your child says **c**, yay! Praise! Hand your child the **c** to hold or place it on the table in view. If they don't say c, give them a little wait time and then give them the answer. Praise them for taking some think time and trying, "Good try!" Then talk about the sound of c and words that start with c. Don't stop there—continue with other two- or three-letter words that each start with a different letter.

You can make this activity about the beginning sound of a word only, or you can continue to the second sound, and then the ending sound. Do your best to keep it easy while you teach. When children really enjoy an activity, they will want to do it again. When you ask if they want to do it again and they say, "Yes," you are right on target.

Activity #8 Going from Letter to Sound
A task for children to see, hear, and do

To go from letter to sound, write out a word that you know your child knows how to read.

For example, if **mom** is a word they know, write out the word **mom** with magnetic letters, but don't say the word. Ask your child to give you the sound to get that word started. If they give you the sound **mmm**, Yay! Be sure to offer praise! If they don't know the sound **mmm**, give them a little wait time and then give them the answer. Praise them for taking the time to think and for trying, "Good try!"

Next, repeat this process with another word that starts with **m**. Then continue with two-letter or three-letter words that start with a different letter. You can make this activity about the beginning sound only, or you can continue to the second sound and then the ending sound. Do your best to keep it easy while you teach. Remember, when children really enjoy an activity, they will want to do it again. When you ask if they want to do it again and they say, "Yes," then you're right on target.

Take Your Time

When you teach in this way, be sure to have fun with these activities and take your time.

First, model the activities, talking aloud about what you are doing and thinking as you model. Then, do the activity together. When children understand how words and letters and reading and writing and talking fit together, and those things become automatic, they will be able to figure out new words on their own. That is what we want. *We want children to know how to help themselves and how to problem solve. We are giving them the tools.*

Remember to praise, praise, praise! Kudos to you for taking the time to gently prepare your children for academics and for giving them processing skills and problem-solving skills, so that they can become independent learners. Nice job!

If you need a quick review on the importance of praise and the best ways to offer it, refer to Chapter I, **Praise Your Child or Shoot Yourself in the Foot.** Yes, it's that important!

CHAPTER Q

Bringing the Workshop to You

"Labor Day is a National Holler Day!"
—*Child, age six*

I attended literacy workshops for 14 years, and one day, right in the middle of a workshop, I began thinking about you. Yes, you! I was sitting there taking notes when it hit me. *Parents might want to know this too!* That's when I decided to write this book.

Now I want to share some of the nuggets of information from those workshops—things that I felt were important enough to write down in my notes.

The Longer I've Worked with Children, the More I Found These to Be True

- **You create the zone**

  Have you ever watched an athlete in the zone? Everything they do looks easy for them and they have perfect timing. Michael Jordan was in the zone in the 1980s and he led his team to an NBA championship. Patrick Mahomes II, quarterback for the Kansas City Chiefs, was in the zone when he led his team to win the Super Bowl.

That's the flow you're looking for when you and your child are doing reading work. Sometimes you will be in the flow, and you'll know it. It will feel really good for both you and your child. Sometimes you won't be in the flow, and that's okay, too. It happens. Don't beat yourself up over it. But the fun, in the flow, focused learning zone is what you are aiming to achieve.

- **Phonics is more for spelling than for reading**
  Phonics is about letters and sounds. It will help you learn to sound out and spell a word. Reading uses letters, sounds, words, phrases, sentences, and meaning.

- **Routine reduces stress**
  Finding a routine for teaching reading reduces stress on you and your child. It makes it easier to focus on something new that we want to add, like reading a new book.

  We all feel more at ease when we are doing something familiar, and we do our best when we have an idea of what to expect.

- **Choice reduces stress**
  It's important to remember you can offer choices that make both you and your child happy.

  "Would you like to wear this shirt or this other shirt?"

  "Would you like to read this book, this book, or this book?"

  "Would you like pancakes or cereal?"

  It's not hard to do!

- **Praise before an activity produces stress**

I had not realized this before hearing it at a workshop, but it is so true in some situations, and it depends on the child. *If we praise before an activity, we set up an expectation that may or may not be met.*

Here's an example: "Katie is so good at reading. Katie, read this book to Grandma and show her how well you read." It's better to simply say, "Katie, would you please read this book to Granma? She likes to listen to you read."

Then, after Katie reads the book, praise her for a job well done.

This website has some good info on praise: https://raisingchildren.net.au/toddlers/videos/good-behaviour-tips-in-action

- **Work and struggle are two different things**
  You want your child to do the work required to learn to read, but you don't want it to be a struggle. That's why it's so important to make learning to read easy and fun for children and to teach them how to easily solve problems for themselves.

- **Appreciate the role of keeping it easy**
  When you keep learning activities easy, there is no struggle. Yes, it can be tricky to teach something new and keep it easy at the same time. One thing to remember is this: You'll know when children are ready for more when your activities and reading go smoothly and seldom require think time. This is not a contradiction to keeping it easy; it's keeping an eye out for a tipping point.

- **Books make language visual**

Children's books have many beautiful illustrations. The illustrations support the meaning of the words in the story. It's a perfect marriage.

- **Learn to let go**
  The movie *Frozen* has certainly brought this expression to light. How does "letting go" apply when learning to read? First, when you sit down to do a mini lesson with your little reader, pick a focus and stick to it. If we try to teach too many things in one lesson, it won't go all that well. *Let go of the things that can be taught at another time and stick to the focus of the lesson at hand.*

- **Memorize when needed**
  Memorize frequently-used words that don't match the sounds we speak. This includes words such as **said, why, which, where.**

- **Contractions**
  When teaching contractions, read out the part before the apostrophe, then sound out the rest. Cover the apostrophe and what comes after it with your finger so your child can see the first part of the word. Then add the part after the apostrophe. For example, if you are teaching the word **can't**, cover the apostrophe and the **t** with your finger so your child can see the word **can**. Then slide your finger to the right and ask your child to sound out the t. Voila! A contraction.

- **"Do you know what smart thing I see you doing?"**
  This is a good thing to say to your child. Why? Because it combines praise with a teaching point.

- **See mistakes as valiant attempts.**
  This is a good mindset to have when someone is trying to learn something new.

- **Keep it active**

  The more that children participate in activities using language, the better readers and writers they become.

  Read to children.

  Talk to children.

  Listen to children.

  And ask questions that evoke answers longer than a yes or a no response. For example: "Why is this your favorite toy?"

  "Why did you choose this book for me to read to you?"

  "Where would you like to sit while we read this book?"

  "Why did you pick this spot to sit and read?"

- **Teach strategies**

  Teach your child how words work and what to do to help themselves when they're stuck.

  Teach how to use the pictures in a book to help with meaning.

Multiple Ways to Learn

Howard Gardner is the author of the Theory of Multiple Intelligences.[4] His work helps teachers better understand children in a classroom. We are all smart in some way.

Help your child learn by figuring out where his or her learning strengths lie, and figure out your own best strategy for teaching. Some people are:

- Word Smart: Communicate by reading, writing, listening, and speaking. Love reading. Learn with language.

- Number Smart: Have an ability to use numbers to solve abstract problems and to reason well. Learn with numbers.

- Body Smart: Use the whole body to express ideas through balance, coordination, dexterity, and strength. Learn through the use of the body.

- Music Smart: Use the elements of tone, rhythm, and pitch. Sensitive to environmental sounds. Learn when ideas are sung or put to rhythm.

- Picture Smart: Have an ability to recreate one's experiences in form, shape, line, color, and texture. Learn through patterns, pictures, and colors.

- Nature Smart: Have an ability to recognize and classify the numerous species of one's environment. Learn from the environment and have an eye for detail.

- People Smart: Have the ability to lead, trust, communicate, and motivate others. Learn by bouncing ideas off others.

- Self Smart: Have the ability to know oneself and assume responsibility for one's life and learning. Learn best with quiet time to think.

Did you recognize your way of learning? Did you recognize your child's way of learning? Each of us is a combination of these smart ways of learning, but we are strongest in one of them. Finding that one, best style of learning is sometimes obvious, but sometimes it takes a while before we recognize it.

No matter what learning style is best for your child, helping them learn to read can be fun, especially when the experience is filled with praise and opportunities for positive results. The problem-solving techniques and experiences that learning to read provide can benefit all aspects of your child's life.

CHAPTER R

Tools and More Tools to Help You Teach Your Child to Read

"I have a pattern in my mouth, tooth,
no tooth, tooth, no tooth."
—Child, age six

My garage is full of tools and, to be honest, I have no idea what half of them are for. I don't know what they're called, and I surely don't know how to use them. I need a manual or better yet a person to tutor me in a one-on-one practical application on how to use these tools, especially the ones I feel confident would make my life easier.

My son gave me a cordless impact driver. I call it a drill. It sits in the garage. I feel happy to have it and I am looking forward to using it someday. I liken the drill in the garage to magnetic letters on the fridge, or children's books sitting on a shelf waiting for a child to learn to read them along with learning to use a whiteboard and markers.

Just as I would like help with learning how to use the tools in my garage, I thought you and your child might like to have one-on-one assistance with how to best use learning-to-read tools. So it was my plan in writing this book to help you use those tools: the magnetic letters, the whiteboard, the markers, the Post-its, children's books, paper, and pencil. This book is a manual for you and you are the manual for your child. I have a few more tools and activities to tell you about.

Another Tool for You

One of my favorite, fun learning-to-read tools is Post-it Labeling and Cover-Up Tape made by 3M. This one-inch-wide tape is white and you can write on it. It sticks to paper, but when you're ready to remove it, it peels off easily. I use Crayola fine-point washable markers to write on it. Note: I use washable markers, because when those little kiddos get hold of a marker, it can miraculously get everywhere.

What to Do with the Tape

Here is one way to use the cover-up tape as a teaching tool. Let's say your child knows five words: **look, see, I, at, and**. Select an appropriate children's book to work with. I chose the board-book version of *The Artist Who Painted a Blue Horse,* by Eric Carle.

Cover all the words in the book with the tape and use markers to write a new story on top of the tape. Use the pictures in the book as your inspiration.

For example, using the words your child knows, write:

Look at the boy.

Look at the horse.

Look at the crocodile.

Look at the cow.

Look at the rabbit.

Look at the lion.

Look at the elephant.

Look at the fox.

Look at the bear.

Look at the donkey.

I like animals. (Give some help with the last line if needed.)

Teach children to use the picture and the sound of the first letter of the animal word to help if they get stuck or if they aren't sure what the animal is.

Use any book you like to rewrite the story on cover-up tape so that children can read it themselves. Get creative: Use what your child knows and add a little something new when you think they're ready.

This idea is a very early learning-to-read activity. You will probably want to do it only a few times, then move on by pulling off the tape and reading the words written by the author.

Use Family Photo Books

A small (4 x 6 inch) photo album with plastic picture pockets can be turned into a wonderful and personal book for your child.

Place pictures connected by a theme in the pockets. For example, put pictures of your dog in the book and then place the cover-up tape on the page with a story to read. Let's say your dog's name is Sammy. Title the book, *Where Is Sammy?*, and create the story on the cover-up tape.

Your story might go something like this:

Sammy is my dog.

Sammy is on the couch.

Sammy is in the yard.

Sammy is on my bed.

Sammy is under the bed.

I love Sammy.

When you mainly use words your child knows, and you tell a story that matches the pictures, you are helping to create a reader who comprehends the story. You are giving your child an opportunity to love reading. It's not too hard, the content is interesting, and it is all at the appropriate level.

Get creative and use these tools in ways that work best for you and your child. You can write the story yourself before introducing it to your child, or you can write the story together in the book.

Your Name on a Book

Here's another idea for a photo book: Use family pictures and words that your child knows. This one has an added bonus—your family name goes on the cover. It's very special when children can see their name written on the cover of a sweet homemade book.

The Shinn Family

I love my papa.

I love my nana.

I love my mom.

I love my baby brother.

I love Sammy.

My family loves me too!

Remember, these books are early learning books. It is my experience that early learning books at this very easy level are difficult to find online, in stores, and at the library. Making your own books simplifies things while personalizing the content.

Reading Books on the Computer Screen

I love technology and it certainly can be a useful tool on the journey toward teaching your child to read. That becomes especially so when your child is ready for e-books. There are websites with learning activities and games as well as books that are read aloud online. However, at the very early stages of learning to read, a computer screen is not the best tool in my opinion. The teaching and learning that I have covered in this book are very hands-on.

I asked a young mother who has a three-year-old and a seven-year-old what she thought of using a tablet to teach her children reading. She said she uses tablets for games and movies but she uses books for reading. Her children love turning pages and looking at the vibrant illustrations. She finds it harder to engage them in reading with a tablet. Using a tablet or a book is a personal preference. Use whatever works best for you and your child.

One Last Tool, a Puzzle Story

Put a banana (or another object) on the table and start a conversation with your child. It will go something like this:

You: "Tommy, what do you see on the table?"

Tommy: "A banana,"

You: "Can you say, 'I see a banana?'"

Tommy: "I see a banana."

- Take a strip of paper, about 1 x 10 inches.

- Write, **I see a banana**. on the strip.

- Ask your child to read it to you. Help with the reading if needed.

- Cut the strip into five pieces (four for the words and one for the period.)

- Mix up the pieces like a puzzle.

- Ask your child to repeat the sentence and then put the sentence back together on the table.

- The period can be separate from the words. This is an opportunity to talk about how a period is a mark that ends a statement.

You will want to model this activity for your child first. After the first round, you can make the story longer. For example:

I see a banana. It is yellow. I like bananas.

In this way you can create little stories together, then cut them into words and put them back together again.

❧

Let's end this book on a fun note! Here are a few more quotes from six-year-old children.

We went to see Snow White and the Seven Doors.

I have a food robot (fruit roll up) for snack.

My pants are in the wrong position. (wedgie)

Squanto spent the night at my house. She's an old friend of my dad's.

I have a big brother and a middle-sized sister.

My sister kicked me in my wrong spot.

My dad is getting his job back on the 35th.

I wish my girlfriend liked me.

It's so hot outside. I'm going to suffercate.

Where do you get a measle shot? Because I'm not going to pull my pants down.

I'm not happy because I don't have a checkbook.

Can I go look in the lost and fountain for my hat?

My brother drowned 20 times already.

Cleaning dishes is better than handwriting.

My mom told me she spent my five dollars on a wild man.

My feet hurt. I've been sleepwalking.

If I wore an earring, I bet they'd let me work at the grocery store.

There's only one petal left and he loves me not.

Learn Something New

To better understand your child on his journey to becoming a reader, learn something new yourself. Learn to play golf, or learn to cook, or learn to play piano, or learn yoga, whatever interests you. Get yourself into a learning situation so you have a feel for what your child is experiencing. It will be good for you and good for your child as you embark on a learning journey together.

Every new learning situation offers opportunities to problem solve. I think it's quite exhilarating to notice a problem and then find a solution. You know that feeling, I'm sure.

Be easy about all of this. Be nice to yourself and be nice to your child. You both deserve to have fun!

"The most beautiful sight in the world is a child walking confidently down a path after you have shown him the way." — Confucius

Endnotes

1   Erica L. Green and Dana Goldstein. "Reading Scores on National
    Exam Decline in Half the States," The New York Times, Updated
    December 5, 2019, https://www.nytimes.com/2019/10/30/us/reading-
    scores-national-exam.html .

2   Mary Anne Doyle. "Communicating the Power of Reading Recovery
    and Literacy Lessons Instruction for Dyslexic Learners: An Ethical
    Response," Journal of Reading Recovery, Spring 2018, https://
    readingrecovery.org/wp-content/uploads/2018/05/jrr_17-2_doyle-2.
    pdf .

3   LoveToKnow, Corp. "Different Learning Styles," Your Dictionary,
    Accessed October 8, 2020, https://education.yourdictionary.com/for-
    teachers/different-learning-styles.html .

4   Howard Gardner. 1983. Frames of mind: the theory of multiple
    intelligences. New York: Basic Books.